52 Michigan Weekends

52 Michigan Weekends

GREAT GETAWAYS AND ADVENTURES FOR EVERY SEASON

THIRD EDITION

BOB PUHALA

COUNTRY ROADS PRESS
NTC/*Contemporary Publishing Group*

Library of Congress Cataloging-in-Publication Data

Puhala, Bob.
    52 Michigan weekends : great getaways and adventures for every
season / Bob Puhala.—3rd ed.
        p.   cm. — (52 weekends)
    Includes index.
    ISBN 1-56626-147-3
    1. Michigan—Guidebooks.   I. Title: Fifty-two Michigan weekends.
II. Title.   III. Series.
F564.3.P84   1999
917.7404'43—dc21   99-051809
                                                                CIP

Cover and interior design by Nick Panos
Cover and interior illustrations copyright © Jill Banashek
Map by Mapping Specialists, Madison, Wisconsin
Picture research by Elizabeth Broadrup Lieberman and Jill Birschbach

Published by Country Roads Press
A division of NTC/Contemporary Publishing Group, Inc.
4255 West Touhy Avenue, Lincolnwood (Chicago), Illinois 60712-1975 U.S.A.
Printed in the United States of America
International Standard Book Number: 1-56626-147-3

00 01 02 03 04 05 QV 19 18 17 16 15 14 13 12 11 10 9 8 7 6 5 4 3 2 1

For Kate and Dayne, my two best Michigan pals; my brother Mark, a primo Wolverine-wandering buddy; and especially my wife, Debbie, who held down the fort. I love you guys!

Contents

Fall

Winter

Introduction

As a little kid growing up in Chicago, I believed that a weekend trip to Michigan was an exotic journey, something so unusual and long distance that it required as much planning as a safari to Africa.

I mean, our family had to cross an ENTIRE state to get there. (Of course, this "entire" state is a small sliver of Indiana. But to a 10-year-old kid and his brother, both possessing vivid imaginations, it was a BIG DEAL!)

So we packed up the family Chevy, pointed it south (it always seemed weird to drive south even though our eventual destination was far north), rumbled past the fouled air of the Gary and Hammond steel mills, and finally arrived in that most foreign of lands—Michigan.

What a world of difference from the steel-and-glass skyscrapers of Chicago, the noisy clangings of El trains in the Loop, and streets crowded with cars and people. Suddenly we were transported into a land of mountainous sand dunes, sleepy harbor villages, seaside resorts, fruit orchards, rocky shorelines—even Mackinac Island, which forbids motor vehicles of all kinds.

Can you imagine? No cars?

Then there was the Upper Peninsula, a land so distant that it seemed like Canada's Northwest Territories to us. Endless forests, ageless mountains, pristine lakes. We thought it was paradise.

Still do. Because today my own girls squeal with delight every time a trip to Michigan is on our travel itinerary. What's the transgenerational appeal?

Despite its reputation as the gritty hub of the nation's automobile manufacturing, large parts of Michigan remain a wilderness virtually unchanged since the first European settlers arrived here.

Four of the Great Lakes nearly surround Michigan, creating a shoreline of more than 3,000 miles—that's longer than the distance from Maine to Florida.

Some of the Midwest's most scenic drives carry travelers from sandy coastal beaches and more than 11,000 inland lakes to 150 waterfalls and 36,000 miles of wild streams.

Then there's the state's rich mining legacies. Vast deposits of iron ore and copper were once unearthed by sweat and industrial ingenuity; visitors can tour several of the old mine shafts.

Lumber barons harvested millions of acres of virgin white pine trees, and though old methods nearly denuded Michigan landscapes in some areas, modern conservation policies have replanted much of that despoliation. In fact, more than 90 percent of the Upper Peninsula has never seen the saw and remains an unbroken tangle of "primeval" forest lands.

That's Michigan's appeal. It's an escape from the pressures of big-city life. A retreat into our historic rural roots. A return to the times when it was a "big deal" to beachcomb for a shiny stone, kick a pinecone along a forest trail, or sit and bask in the eternal wonder of a beautiful sunset.

And that's my Michigan. Along with Detroit's Motown sound. Dearborn's Henry Ford Museum. Flint's Buick City. Battle Creek's "world's longest cereal table." Pontiac's Silverdome. Ypsilanti's Yankee Air Museum. Niles's Fernwood Botanical Gardens. L'Anse's Shrine of the Snowshoe Priest. Hancock's copper mines. Cheboygan's opera house. Grand Rapids's Gerald Ford Museum. Jackson's Ella Sharp Homestead Museum.

And lots more.

Hope you enjoy the Wolverine State as much as I do.

Spring

1

Hey, Dude!

ROTHBURY

THREE "STEEPLECHASE" RACERS, LOCKED ARM-IN-ARM, ARE
running through an obstacle course inside the main corral.
The middle one is blindfolded by a colorful bandanna.

Not a big deal until you realize that this wacky cowboy
contest doesn't end until his partners get him to jump over
a mountainous pile of steaming horse manure without
pulling them all down into the smelly goo.

Watching that spectacle, I decided that this was the most
fun I'd had at a dude ranch in quite a while.

Or maybe I decided when the head wrangler led us, galloping full tilt on horseback, across an open meadow in a
scene straight out of a Clint Eastwood western.

Then again, it might have been at the rifle range, where I
plugged three bull's-eyes in five shots, and my wife, Debbie, managed one sharp shot herself. Our success with
firearms was not totally surprising for a couple of gun-
slingers from Chicago, a city wilder than any Wild West cow
town ever was.

These cowboy adventures are all part of the action at the
Double JJ Resort in Rothbury, an adults-only dude ranch covering 1,200 acres on Michigan's Lower Peninsula, about 20
miles north of Muskegon.

But the Double JJ is more than just a cowpoke mecca. Think of it as an affordable North Woods "Club Med," boasting some of the friendliest staff this side of the Pecos (some from as far away as Australia) and fun-loving regular guests (mostly from around Detroit, Chicago, and Windsor, Ontario) who treat newcomers like part of one big, happy family.

The atmosphere at the ranch is casual, and guests can do as much or as little as they like. Besides daily trail rides, there are barbecue cookouts, hayrides, and sing-alongs; archery and rifle ranges; tennis and volleyball courts; a heated swimming pool and an outdoor hot tub; a private lake with beach, paddleboats, rowboats, and canoes; and nightly entertainment that includes live bands, DJs, karaoke, and stage shows.

Traditional ranch rooms don't vary much in decor or layout from other dude ranches across the country: bed (double or bunks), reading lamps, and private bath. Deluxe ranch rooms offer queen-size beds, a mini-fridge, and a coffee machine.

You can also opt for one of the Homestead's luxury condos that face the challenging new 18-hole course at the Thoroughbred Golf Club, part of an ongoing multimillion-dollar expansion project that also includes the Loft, offering upscale hotel rooms, and a conference center.

The Double JJ excels, though, in its riding program; it painstakingly matches individual riding skills with one of the ranch's 60-plus horses.

The "walk ride" is a pleasant four-legged stroll for beginners. Intermediates go on a rump-busting romp that includes plenty of trotting and cantering. Advanced rides might have sufficed to train Pony Express riders. On one excursion, the trail guide even gave us some tips that few dude ranch cowboys ever mention, almost immediately improving our horseback skills.

The next day we were turned over to the head wrangler. "I don't tell dirty jokes or flirt with the women," the taciturn cowboy told us. "I just flat-out ride. So let's get with the program, kids."

Ride we did, at a gallop for nearly half of our hour's ride in what came close to being an advanced session. It also was the best pure horse riding Debbie and I have experienced, and that includes visits to hard-core dude ranches in Colorado and Wyoming.

The ranch is noted for its theme weeks. A favorite is Old West Week, which boasts a daylong horseback ride to nearby Lake Michigan, where the Double JJ chuck wagon awaits with a barbecue lunch served on bluff-top sand dunes. My favorite is Labor Week, usually held the first week of September, when everybody (including guests) works a day as a ranch hand, helping to prepare the spread for the coming cold weather. For their efforts, guests receive a substantial discount off lodging rates.

You also can enjoy special weekends throughout the year, which feature everything from fall-color rides (truly spectacular autumn scenery abounds in these parts) to country-and-western extravaganzas that'll have you singing cowboy tunes faster than you can say Garth Brooks.

Hey Dude!

FOR MORE INFORMATION

The Double JJ Resort is open daily mid-May through late September, then weekends through October. Rates include two-night weekends, three-night mini-vacations, and entire weeks; included are three meals a day, lodging, taxes, and ranch activities. Call 616-894-4444.

2

Bicycling the Wolverine State

THE RUGGED TRAILS OF MICHIGAN'S ROCKY LAKESHORES, THE lonely farm roads skirting its expansive vineyards, the rolling hills of its Fruit Belt, and the rough off-road paths leading to the state's craggy mountaintops are perfect for bicycle tours filled with adventure and spectacular scenery.

That's probably why Michael and Libby Robold founded Michigan Bicycle Touring, which has specialized in guided outdoor cycling vacations for almost 20 years.

It's been said that Mike and Libby have checked out every lighthouse harbor, every lake, every berry-picking, wildflower-waving, fudge-munching corner of Michigan to bring cycle fans the best outdoor adventures. As a result, they (and their staff) know the best routes for safety, ability, and scenery.

MBT trips offer lodging and meals in everything from charming lakeside inns and historic lodges to deluxe resorts. Cyclists can choose from several routes of varying lengths every day, with shorter, less-demanding trails designed for beginners. They also can sign up for optional hikes, canoe trips, and other along-the-trail activities.

However, it's not all biking and hiking. Afternoons and evenings are often filled with swimming, beachcombing—or simply relaxing.

You don't have to be in top shape to join in the cycling fun. In fact, most of the time, you just need to know how to ride a bike. People of all ages and abilities sign up for MBT's bike tours, with a typical range from the mid-20s to near–senior citizens. The average bike tour size is 15. Tour leaders are trained in everything from group dynamics and roadside repairs to meal-making and luggage handling.

MBT offers weekend tours and five-day trips covering the state's most compelling scenery. Here are some tour highlights:

Weekend Tours

Pentwater Amble   This bike tour winds around Pentwater Lake before challenging the hilly inland roads leading into quaint towns such as Mears, New Era, and Rothbury. A highlight is the Gemstone Factory in Shelby, which sells sparkling manmade diamonds, emeralds, and rubies. You'll also explore the northern shore of Lake Michigan and other lakeside trails. A favorite stop is White Pine Village, a 19th-century living-history hamlet with costumed interpreters, pioneer crafts, and special events.

Mackinac Islander   The eight-mile-long highway that rings this rock, resting in the straits between Lakes Michigan and Huron, is open only to bicycle traffic. So it's a perfect place to explore the island's wondrous natural rock formations, the lush green woods of Bois Blanc, and Fort Holmes—the rock's highest point and best spot for viewing spectacular sunsets. When you're not plying the island's outer reaches, pedal into town (there are no motor vehicles allowed on the island, except for emergency crews) to see turn-of-the-century architecture; take a horse-drawn carriage ride; and visit Fort Mackinac, populated by "Colonial soldiers" who demonstrate musket firing and other drills.

And I dare you to resist buying some melt-in-your-mouth goodies at one of the island's numerous fudge shops.

Platte River Pedal & Paddle   First you'll paddle down the gentle Platte River, a shallow, crystal-clear stream that meanders peacefully through pristine wilderness. There's a catered gourmet picnic on the afternoon's menu. Later you'll pedal through hilly terrain along Crystal Lake. And you'll enjoy performances at the renowned Interlochen Center for the Arts, where students from every state and 30 countries study each summer. Programs include classical music, dance, and theater productions.

Mendon Amble   Dinner in the home of a local Amish family is the highlight of this tour, which rambles through the buggy-dotted hills of Michigan's Amish country. It also includes a ride over the 1887 Langley Covered Bridge, one of Michigan's few remaining covered bridges; a visit to Colon, "Magic Capital of the World" and home to Abbott's Magic Manufacturing Company, which produces more than 2,000 magic tricks and gadgets; and an optional canoe trip on the St. Joseph River.

Five-Day Tours

Lake Superior Wilderness Trek   Mountain biking at its best, this tour winds through unspoiled wilderness providing breakneck off-road fun. Woodland trails dissect unbroken forests, many leading into the vast Huron Mountains. Special afternoon outings include canoeing, kayaking, and nature hikes that reveal hidden rivers and waterfalls. You'll overnight at Big Bay Point Lighthouse, built in 1896 on a rocky cliff overlooking Lake Superior. It's one of only two lighthouses operating as bed-and-breakfasts in the United States, and supposedly features a ghost that jangles chains in the dead of night.

Tahquamenon Wayfarer This Upper Peninsula idyll includes rides along three lakes (Michigan, Huron, and Superior); views of Tahquamenon Falls, at 48 feet the second highest waterfall east of the Mississippi River; a visit to the 1849 Whitefish Point Lighthouse, oldest active light on Lake Superior; and an optional four-mile hike along a wilderness river trail. You'll also visit Sault Ste. Marie, on the Canadian border; take a boat cruise through the famous Soo Locks; and tour the SS *Valley Camp*, a retired iron ore carrier.

Porcupine Mountain Wayfarer This is an intensive hike-and-bike tour that includes two days of trekking trails in the Porcupine Mountains, a 58,000-acre wilderness tract on the westernmost tip of the Upper Peninsula. For example, during a four-mile hike, you'll climb the Escarpment Trail's challenging, rugged, and sometimes steep terrain, including numerous crossings of the Little Carp River; on an 11-mile trek, relatively level ground yields peeks at several waterfalls, stands of huge virgin pine trees, and cascading rapids on the Little Carp. You'll also cycle the Porkies, pedaling over glacial ridges and hills into Black Canyon, home to towering evergreens, wild rivers, rocky ridges, and eight waterfalls.

For More Information

Reservations must be made for all MBT bike tours. Prices include all lodging, breakfasts, dinners, gratuities for inns, taxes, trip leader services, roadside repairs, canoe rentals, ferry trips, maps, and luggage transportation (for five-day tours only). Picnic lunches are included in five-day tours and special weekend trips. Children's rates (ages nine to seventeen) are available. A lightweight touring bike is recommended for "regular" tours; mountain bikes with 15 speeds or more are required for off-road trips. Both can be rented from MBT, along with helmets (which are mandatory).

Contact Michigan Bicycle Touring Inc., 3512 Red School Road, Kingsley, MI 49649, 616-263-5885.

Biegeling the Wolverine State

3

Morelizing in Michigan

WALLOON LAKE

EVERY SPRING, MICHIGAN IS INVADED BY A HALF-MILLION fanatics. Dressed in baggy old clothes and armed with sticks and paper bags, they wander through swamps, forests, and meadows and along rivers in what appears to be a bizarre ritual pursued by nature lovers who have lost their sense of direction.

What are these people looking for?

The morel, a tiny sponge-like fungus that some call the most delicious and elusive of all wild mushrooms, prized in kitchens and included on menus of the world's most famous restaurants.

Unfortunately, morels are difficult to find. And for the careless or uneducated morel hunter, harvesting the wrong wild mushroom could be deadly.

To learn the difference between safe and nasty morels and still experience the thrill of the hunt, consider joining a "Morels and More" weekend at Springbrook Hills Resort in Walloon Lake, about 50 miles north of Traverse City.

For five consecutive weekends each spring (from mid-April through late May), Springbrook owner Joe Breidenstein and morel expert Larry Lonik teach guests how to hunt and cook this fabulous fungus. The fun includes a Saturday night steak cookout featuring morel dishes prepared by experienced morel chefs.

"Actually, the morel is the easiest wild mushroom to identify and the safest to pick if you know what to look for," Lonik said. "Nothing else that grows in hardwood forests looks like it."

Easy for Lonik to say. This morel-meister, now in his mid-40s, has been hunting the delicacy since he was six years old. "The first time my dad took me out, it felt like a giant Easter egg hunt," he said. "It still does."

Lonik isn't alone in his obsession. Nearly 10 million morel hunters in North America tramp through damp woods every spring searching for the funny-looking fungus.

Morels taste "like sirloin steak," the expert swears. "They have a meaty flavor, are delicious in soups and quiches, and contain no calories."

Of course, morel hunters (especially first-timers) need an experienced guide to point out differences between edible and dangerous morels. Of the 200,000 species of wild mushrooms that grow throughout the world, nearly 80 are picked for cooking; about 40, including the "Destroying Angel," are known to be deadly. In the United States, about five mushroom-related deaths are reported each year.

"Once I identify a safe morel for inexperienced pickers, they should have few problems staying away from questionable ones," Lonik said.

Activities during Springbrook's annual morel weekends include a mushroom identification slide show led by Lonik, a 90-minute group hunt, time to search the woods on your own, and an evening steak dinner and morel-cooking demonstration featuring Lonik's recipes. His morel quiche is said to be so good it's often served as dessert.

Guests staying at Springbrook during Mother's Day weekend often receive another bonus: a trip to nearby Boyne City's National Mushroom Hunting Festival.

Springbrook's Breidenstein and Lonik also have cooked up another interesting first: midweek morel hunting on horseback during May. "Going three or four miles into the backwoods on horseback and finding a patch of morels nobody has ever gotten to is like discovering a gold mine," Breidenstein said.

Literally. Area roadside morel stands sell freshly picked fungus for as much as $15 or $20 per pound. Sought-after dried morels can fetch nearly $350 per pound.

Don't expect morel hunting to be singular and solitary unless you opt for the horseback hunt. "In good picking years, cars, campers, and vans will be lined bumper-to-bumper on tiny backcountry roads," Breidenstein said. "You might spot license plates from as far away as West Virginia and Florida."

For More Information

"Morels and More" weekend packages at Springbrook Hills Resort include two nights' lodging in a vacation home with fireplace, Friday-night party, stocked refrigerators for Saturday and Sunday breakfasts, wine tasting, and all morel activities. Guided horseback morel hunts include Monday- and Tuesday-night lodging and all other activities. Contact Springbrook Hills Resort, P.O. Box 219, Walloon Lake, MI 49796, 616-535-2227.

Morelizing in Michigan

4

Tulip Time

HOLLAND

UNLIKE MANY OTHER MIDWESTERNERS WHO PRAY FOR OLD man winter to end, people in Holland pray for a long and lingering cold season.

No, they aren't goofy. It's just that nasty weather means perfect blooming conditions and peak colors for the annual Tulip Time Festival in Holland.

Held in early May, Tulip Time continues to be one of the Midwest's most wildly popular events, drawing nearly one million people each spring to this little town founded by Dutch immigrants more than 150 years ago. Three huge parades, klompen (wooden shoe) dancers, street scrubbers, historic-house walks, and wooden-shoe-factory tours are part of the Dutch-style fun. But millions of blossoming tulips remain the fest's main attraction.

The easiest way to see the blooms is to get into your car and tour eight miles of Tulip Lanes winding along Holland streets. The tulip fields, which start at Twelfth Street and River Avenue, are planted with more than 50 varieties. There also are special plantings in the park at Eighth Street and Lincoln Avenue.

If you'd rather not drive, hop aboard downtown's Tulip Trolley, which crosses Tulip Lanes, city parks, and other Dutch heritage sites. The 75-minute tours, departing from the fest's Civic Center headquarters, are led by a Dutch-costumed guide who shares insights about Holland's ethnic culture and history.

Another tulip hot spot is Windmill Island, two miles (and two centuries) from downtown. There stands DeZwaan, the nation's only working Dutch windmill. The 200-year-old windmill is 12 stories high with sails spanning 80 feet. DeZwaan is a splendid setting for more than 100,000 tulips flowering in Windmill Island's gardens. Admission is charged. Call 616-396-5433.

You can enjoy some of Holland's most beautiful tulip displays at Veldheer's Tulip Gardens, north of town on U.S. 31 and Quincy Street. Millions of tulips bloom in brilliant colors amid the gardens' setting of windmills, drawbridges, and canals. You can even buy tulip bulbs for your own garden. Admission is charged. Call 616-399-1900.

Other top town attractions include:

Spring

- The New Holland Museum, which boasts Dutch decorative arts, delftware, pewter, and antique furniture. Admission is charged. Call 616-392-9084.

- Dutch Village, a 15-acre re-created turn-of-the-century Holland hamlet with canals, bridges, tulip gardens, wooden-shoed dancers, ethnic museum, historic farmhouse, and more. Admission is charged. Call 616-396-1475.

- Wooden Shoe Factory, where craftspeople hand-shape clunky shoes from logs on antique machines. You can get your own pair personalized, or you can watch delftware being hand-painted. Admission is free. Call 616-396-6513.

Annual Tulip Time festival highlights include:

- Tours of the Cappon House, an 1874 Victorian eight-room house that belonged to Holland's first mayor. Admission is charged. Call 616-392-6740.

- Volksparade, on Eighth Street between Columbia and Kollen Park, which is preceded by the town crier's announcement that the "streets are too dirty for a public event"—or at least not up to standards of Dutch cleanliness. This is followed by a brigade of costumed street scrubbers with pails swinging from shoulder yokes; they splash the pavement until the two-hour-long parade begins.

- Children's Costume Parade, beginning at Columbia and Eighth. Reserved bleacher seats are available for the two-hour celebration for a small fee.

- The grand Parade of Bands, which wraps up Tulip Time fun. It struts its stuff (which includes scores of horn-filled marching bands, klompen dancers, and other paraders in ethnic Dutch costumes) on Eighth Street from Columbia to Van Ralte, south to Twenty-Fourth Street. There's also a Tulip Time Water Ski Show later that evening at Kollen Park.

Tulip Time

For More Information

Contact Holland Area Convention & Visitors Bureau, 171 Lincoln Avenue, Holland, MI 49423, 616-396-4221 or, outside Michigan, 800-822-2770.

5

Duffer's Paradise

MICHIGAN GOLF

I'M HEADING NORTH THIS SUMMER TO THE GOLF COAST FOR a little "green magic."

That's the "G-O-L-F" Coast—3,200 miles of Great Lakes shoreline in Michigan, which boasts some 10,000 holes of golf, maybe more than any other state.

In fact, Michigan is staking its claim as America's summer golf capital. Statistics show that people play more rounds of golf in the Great Lakes area than in any other region of the country. Michigan alone has more than 600 public golf courses, including some of the finest municipal links (the Grand Haven Municipal course is rated in the nation's top 75 by *Golf Digest*) and fabulous "designer courses" built by golf legends Jack Nicklaus and Arnold Palmer.

Couple those statistics with the fact that Michigan is one of the nation's top 10 travel destinations, with world-class resorts, freshwater fishing, swimming, sailing, and historic attractions all among the vacation possibilities, and you have the makings of a holiday haven that offers plenty of fun to golfers and nongolfers alike.

But spring has sprung, and we're talking golf—the "thwack" of the ball booming far off the tee, hitting irons out of knee-high rough, water hazards, sand traps the size of Delaware, three-putt greens, penalty strokes—well, now you know a little bit about my golf game.

Let's take a swing through Michigan, and you'll see how the state is earning a reputation as the golf mecca of the Midwest.

Antrim Dells Golf Club, Atwood Golfers here are treated to what seems like two entirely different courses. The front nine plays long, with flat, open fairways, twin bunkers guarding every green, and little water. It's a good opportunity to "muscle up" on your swing without too much worry about accuracy. But the course's transformation on the back nine is stunning. Suddenly, accuracy is a major concern, with Michigan's famous hardwood trees to contend with on virtually every shot. They line tees, guard narrow fairways, and seem to surround greens.

Number 10 demands that you drive your ball from an elevated tee directly into a tree-infested fairway. There's no respite on number 12, a 543-yard par 5. Its fairway is lined on both sides with more trees; you have to zigzag your way around them, losing distance as you veer away from the woods. Water on the left side of the fairway causes more mind games for golfers with fragile egos and wild strokes. The back nine's unholy trio is completed with number 13, an extremely difficult 170-yard par 3 that serves as the course's signature hole. Your drive from an elevated tee must carry over water, yet land between two large sand traps and short of another that guards the back of the green. The view from the tee is breathtaking, but all the open space allows swirling winds to further complicate your drive. Call 800-872-8561.

The Legend at Shanty Creek, Bellaire This Arnold Palmer–designed course stretches nearly 7,000 yards from the championship tees, snaking through mountains, ravines, tall Michigan hardwoods, five lakes, creeks, and a cedar swamp. There's not a dull hole to be found. In fact, it was named by *Golf Digest* as Michigan's number-one resort course.

Each hole is almost self-contained in a "private" environmental amphitheater; there are no adjoining fairways, and the rolling up-and-down mountain terrain is surrounded by thick woods. No matter how crowded the course may be, you'll rarely see another person outside your foursome.

You'll be awed by the 496-yard par-5 first hole, which challenges with its tree-locked fairway. Number seven, another par 5, is even more spectacular, with its green tucked into a hillside and fronted by the shimmering waters of Shanty Creek. Call 800-678-4111.

A-Ga-Ming Golf Club, Kewadin   A-Ga-Ming (an American Indian word meaning "beside the lake") overlooks the hypnotic blue waters of Torch Lake, named by *National Geographic* magazine as one of the 10 most beautiful lakes in the country. Chick Harbert, the 1954 PGA champion, is the director of golf at this 6,500-yard par-72 course.

The front nine is the older layout, with rolling fairways framed by woods and soft, level greens. Number one, a 394-yard par 4, serves up a dogleg right with an elevated fairway hanging high above a sunken green. Woods and a pond fronting the green add to the challenge.

On the recently opened back nine, water, sharp doglegs, even a cherry orchard add to the thrills. A favorite is the 198-yard par-3 17th hole that provides a beautiful vista of Torch Lake. The view is especially spectacular in the fall when Michigan's hardwoods are ablaze with fiery colors. Call 616-264-5081.

"Tree Tops" at Sylvan Resort   Located near Gaylord, this is Robert Trent Jones's masterpiece, with the links cutting

Duffer's Paradise

through dense woods in the picturesque Sturgeon River Valley. It is awesomely beautiful in autumn.

Jones, a world-renowned golf course architect, was inspired to call this up-and-down "mountain" course Tree Tops because of the view from the par-3 number-six hole. An elevated tee offers a view of more than 20 miles of Michigan hardwoods; it also looks down to a small green that demands accuracy. Call 517-732-6711.

Michaywe Hills Golf Club, near Gaylord This is arguably the best-maintained course in the state, with pinewood forests secluding each hole from the next, numerous bunkers and sand traps, and greens that are absolutely flawless. You're also likely to see an abundance of wildlife on the course during early morning or dusk. A friend told me he has seen a fox running across the fairway, along with rabbits, deer, and wild turkey. Call 517-939-8911.

Crystal Mountain, near Thompsonville *Travel Weekly Magazine* has rated Crystal Mountain one of the world's most beautiful resort courses. It's heavily wooded with lots of water (trouble on about 10 holes), and birch, beech, and cedar draped among rolling fairways manicured to resemble plush green carpets. The small, undulating greens are elegant, and the feeling of isolation and solitude is especially attractive. Call 616-378-2911.

Schuss Mountain, near Mancelona It has been called "one of the Midwest's finest 18 holes of championship golf" by *Golf Traveler Magazine*. There are about 14 tree-lined fairways that manage to play wide open, and huge greens. Another special touch is the strategically placed trout-filled ponds lining the 18th fairway. The course has an astounding 120 acres of maintained turf; compare that with about 30 acres at a world-renowned course like Florida's Sawgrass.

Needless to say, this mountain course is immensely popular. Call 616-533-8621.

Boyne Highlands' Heather and Moor courses, near Harbor Springs Each course boasts nine holes designed by Robert Trent Jones. Heather has been rated one of the nation's "Top 100" courses by *Golf Digest* for more than a decade. The marshlands lining the course have earned it a reputation for toughness, and you must be accurate with your shots to succeed here. The Moor is a flatter course, but lots of sand, water, and tree-lined fairways demand good shot placement. Call 616-549-2441.

Boyne Mountain's "The Monument" course, East Jordan Designed by renowned architect William Newcomb, it stretches nearly 7,100 yards from the top of Michigan's most famous ski mountain, along magnificent meadows, until finally reaching the shores of Deer Lake.

The first hole offers a spectacular elevated tee on the apex of Boyne Mountain, 1,300 feet above the green. It has a sharp dogleg right (so sharp the fairway is banked) that seems to plow right through dense woods; it feels like you've hit your tee shot down a long funnel, and that it'll roll forever to the green.

The course's other attention grabber is number 18, The Island Hole. The 460-yard par 4 is surrounded by water (connected to the fairway by a tiny bridge) with the green further guarded by a large sand trap.

The Monument eventually will have holes named for the world's most famous golfers, but owner Edmund Kirchers is in no hurry since he contends

Duffer's Paradise

that a number of the world's golf greats have yet to be born. Call 616-549-2441.

The Bear, Grand Traverse Bay   No story about the Golf Coast would be complete without a mention of the Bear, perhaps the region's most-talked-about links. The Jack Nicklaus–designed course, which hosted the 1990 PGA Senior Open, winds its way along cherry orchards with the placid blue waters of Grand Traverse Bay stretching along the horizon. But don't let all this marvelous scenery lull you into a false sense of bliss. This is an 18-hole golf survival test. Fairways are riddled with mounds, county-size bunkers, and all kinds of woods and water. Especially fetching (translated: have another sleeve of new balls handy) is the par-3 13th hole that vexes with a fairway sliced in two by a rambling creek, traps so deep you need ladders to climb out of them, and a two-tiered green. Call 800-748-0303.

Other quick picks:

• **The Rock on Drummond Island**   The course has been blasted out of this Lake Huron island's limestone foundation to create a real challenge—not only for its seven water holes, but wandering hazards like white-tailed deer, foxes, even a bear or two. Call 906-493-1026.

• **Elk Ridge Golf Course in Atlanta**   Named runner-up for *Golf Digest*'s "best new public course in 1991," wildly challenging terrain includes a duck marsh, trout stream, lakes, wetlands, huge elk hanging around the par-4 number sixteen—and a pig-shaped bunker on number 10 (an inside joke for founder Lou Schmidt, owner of Honey Baked Ham). Call 800-626-4355.

- **Garland Resort in Lewiston** Fifty-four fairways wind through 3,000 acres of dense forest, with rugged swamps, dense trees, and rolling terrain. There's also a par-36, nine-hole walking course that's a real teaser. Call 517-786-2211.

For More Information

Michigan resorts and courses offer everything from daily greens fees to ultimate golf vacation packages on courses designed by some of the world's most renowned golf architects and with lodging at select world-class resorts. Packages may include lodging, golf, prearranged tee times, greens fees each day, electric cart, and taxes. Call the individual resort listed above, or contact Michigan Travel Bureau, P.O. Box 3393, Lansing, MI 48151, 800-543-2937.

Duffer's Paradise

6

When Irish Eyes Are Smiling

CLARE

'TIS A GREAT DAY TO BE WEARIN' O' THE GREEN, ST. PATRICK'S Day is. The nation's—and Michigan's—lads and lassies proudly don the colors of Auld Sod, heralding their rich ethnic heritage with parades and celebrations.

Of course, you don't have to be Irish to celebrate St. Paddy's. This is the one day of the year when everybody's invited to recognize the leprechaun that's inside of them, screaming to come out—or to at least sing the Notre Dame fight song.

Before we go on a little bit more, now, it'd be good to know a wee bit of the man of the hour—St. Patrick, himself.

In the year 410, when Patrick was a lad of about 16, he was kidnapped by Irish pirates off the western coast of Britain and carried to Ireland to be a slave. Patrick remained there, doing the bidding of his masters (the people who would one day be his own spiritual children), until he miraculously escaped to France six years later.

He eventually made his way home to Britain, but had a desire to bring to his captors the faith that sustained him in his captivity. So Patrick returned to France (his mother's brother was St. Martin of Tours), became a priest and a bishop—and returned to Ireland as a missionary.

Though his life was often threatened as he faced hardships in the pagan land that was Ireland, Patrick persevered, laboring among "barbarians" and ridiculed by other Catholic bishops who thought Patrick would fail because of his lack of formal learning.

But all were astonished when his spirit so moved the Irish people that they converted to Catholicism. Legend has Patrick driving all the snakes (a symbol of the devil) out of Ireland, healing people, and fasting atop Mt. Aigli for 40 days and 40 nights. It was from that hill that Patrick blessed all the people of Ireland—both of his time and of all generations to come.

And the Irish people came to love him, calling him the "Apostle of Ireland." He is credited with converting an entire nation, which demonstrates the power of one good person when he is rooted in God's love.

And let's not forget St. Patrick's most famous legend—how he used the shamrock (three-leafed clover) to explain the Holy Trinity, a foundational belief of Roman Catholicism, to Irish pagans.

Of course, the Puhala family celebrates St. Patrick bigtime, mainly because my mother's family (Smith/McGowan) comes from County Armagh, where Patrick's church is located and where the saint is buried. And yes, corned beef, cabbage, Irish potatoes, soda bread, and pints of Guinness are standards on our St. Patrick's dinner table.

And that's no blarney.

If you want to celebrate St. Patrick's day yourself, keeping green from morning to night, follow these suggestions leading to your pot o' gold. They lead to Irish step dancers, hornpipes, and bagpipes, all part of the fun during the annual Clare Irish Festival, a mid-March bash in Clare. That it takes an entire week to cram in all the activities that celebrate Ireland's patron saint should be no surprise—especially after you realize that the town is named after Auld Sod's County Clare.

Irish eyes will be smiling on everyone during the Green Day bash, one of the largest and longest in the Midwest. Listen to traditional Irish folk and fiddle music; see distinctly Irish arts and crafts; dance to a jig or reel; and even sample a bit of Irish stew.

And remember, lads and lassies who eye each other across the dance floor: No patty-fingers, the both of ya.

FOR MORE INFORMATION

Call the Clare Chamber of Commerce, 517-386-2442.

31

When Irish Eyes Are Smiling

7

Wheeling Around the Motor City

DETROIT

WHETHER YOUR IMAGE OF DETROIT IS THE GLEAMING skyscrapers of downtown's futuristic Renaissance Center or the gritty neighborhoods of a despoiled Rust Belt city, there's still plenty here for visitors to enjoy on a weekend ramble of the nation's eighth-largest metropolitan area.

Of course, you'll need a car in "the town that Ford built" to get around and see all the sights. Maybe you'll even want to head out of town, going south to Canada, eh? So buckle up your seat belt and get ready to wheel around the Motor City.

A good place to start is the Renaissance Center, whose massive steel-and-glass tower rises above the Detroit River next to the tunnel leading into Canada. The controversial two-million-square-foot office and store complex has been heralded by supporters as a symbol of the city's rebirth (following the destructive 1967 Detroit riots); critics have called it a "fortress intended to protect its occupants from neighboring vandals."

Besides shops and eateries, the 73-story skyscraper provides fantastic vistas of the island-dotted Detroit River, Lake St. Clair, and Windsor, Canada. Take an elevator ride up to the observation lounge or enjoy a meal at the Center's Summit Steak House, a revolving restaurant on the 72nd floor. Call 313-568-5600.

Keep your car in that parking lot for just a little while longer and hop aboard the People Mover, a $200-million rail system that runs a three-mile loop through the heart of downtown Detroit. Thirteen stops along the route offer a panorama of downtown highlights, including Bricktown, Grand Circus Park, and the river. The entire loop takes about 15 minutes. It's quite safe, clean, and regularly patrolled. Call 313-962-7245.

Hart Plaza, the city's riverfront amphitheater, offers free music and delicious ethnic treats almost every summer weekend. For current events schedules, call 313-224-1184.

Rev up your engines and motor to Greektown, a frenetic block on Monroe Street that recalls 19th-century Detroit with its restored buildings and lively around-the-clock nightlife. Besides Greek stores, bakeries, coffeehouses, and restaurants (where you can sample great homemade egg-lemon soup, souvlaki, and more), the main Greektown attraction is Trappers Alley. Located in a historic four-story tannery complex, the festive marketplace boasts all kinds of specialty shops, art galleries, Greek bakeries, and grocery stores where you can buy a fabulous Greek dry red wine. Call 313-963-5445.

During baseball season, I cannot pass through Detroit without taking in a baseball game at Tiger Stadium (about one mile west of downtown on Michigan Avenue). Only the Cubs' Wrigley Field and Boston's Fenway Park can compare to this historic 1912 gem; it also boasts the best upper-deck seats in the majors, where fans seem to hover over the outfielders. In fact, I almost caught a Cecil Fielder home run in the left-field upper deck about two years ago. For tickets, call 313-258-4437.

I heard it through the grapevine that a visit to the Motown Historical Museum on West Grand Boulevard will have you dancing in the streets. Actually, the museum was Motown Records' first recording studio. In its heyday, the likes of Smokey Robinson and the Miracles, the Supremes, and the Temptations made music here. Forty-five-minute tours include a musician's gallery featuring everything from Stevie Wonder's first harmonica to an entire room dedicated to Michael Jackson, who was 10 years old when he first recorded for Motown. Call 313-875-2264.

To escape Detroit's urban muscle, head to Belle Isle, called "one of the most beautiful urban parks in the world." Located on a 1,000-acre island, the park offers the oldest public aquarium in the United States, a zoo, a nature center, guided hikes, canoe rides, the Great Lakes Museum and working lighthouse, a conservatory, and more. Views into Canada are spectacular, and spray from the ornate Scott Fountain splashes nearly 80 feet into the air. Call 313-267-7115.

For a glimpse of how the city's auto barons lived, tour their elegant estates (see Chapter 39). They include Edsel Ford's 87-acre Grosse Pointe Shores estate overlooking Lake St. Clair, a luxurious English Cotswold–style mansion that remains unchanged since Ford died in 1947; call 313-884-3400. Lawrence Fisher's dazzling 50-room Detroit mansion comes complete with majolica tiles with gold insets, Corinthian columns, and gold and silver leaf on ceilings and moldings; call 313-331-6740. Meadow Brook Hall, a 100-room Tudor mansion in Rochester, was built by the widow of John Dodge; call 313-370-3140.

History buffs shouldn't miss Historic Fort Wayne, on Jefferson Avenue just off 1-75. The 83-acre military complex, with an encircling moat and 22-foot-tall walls, includes the original 1840 barracks and tunnels, gun towers, restored

Civil War–era buildings, and a museum chronicling Detroit's military history, starting with the French in 1701 through the Indian Wars of the 1890s. Due to budget cuts, the fort is open only during a few special events. Call 313-833-1805.

If you want to enjoy Detroit's biggest bash, visit during the annual Freedom Festival, June 22–July 4 (see Chapter 28). This massive celebration stretches across the border into Windsor, Ontario, commemorating both Canada Day (July 1) and our nation's Independence Day (July 4). Activities include the nation's only parade that winds through two countries, a massive fireworks display, hydroplane races in the Detroit River, and other activities. Call 313-887-8200.

Take the Ambassador Bridge or the International Tunnel south into Windsor, Ontario, home to more than 900 acres of beautiful parks, public gardens with more than 500 varieties of roses, and the world's only fountain floating in international waters. You'll note its French-Canadian influences, and you can enjoy its symphony, light opera, and theaters, or visit its North American Black Historical Museum, which traces the achievements of many black people who fled the United States to Canada on the Underground Railroad. Call 519-256-2641.

Places to overnight? The Renaissance Center tower's Westin Hotel guest rooms claim the best panoramic city views as well as peeks across the river into Canada. Call 313-568-8000.

History-lovers might choose a room at the Dearborn Inn, a 222-room hotel built in 1931 by Henry Ford. The inn offers both Colonial Williamsburg furnishings in "regular" rooms and a Colonial-style "village on the green," where you can stay in historical replicas of the homes homes of Edgar Allan Poe, Patrick Henry, and others. Call 313-271-2700.

Bed-and-breakfast fans could opt for the Blanche House Inn, a charming turn-of-the-century residence that resembles a mini–White House in its exterior construction. The guest house (14 rooms, all with private bath) once served as a private school for boys; Henry Ford II is one of its alumni. Call 313-822-7090.

For More Information

Contact Metropolitan Detroit Convention and Visitors Bureau, 100 Renaissance Center, Suite 1950, Detroit, MI 48243, 800-338-7648.

Wheeling Around the Motor City

8

Angling for a Whopper

FISHING MICHIGAN

ANGLING FOR THAT MONSTER LUNKER TAKES PATIENCE, SKILL, and expert advice on finding those mind-boggling fishing holes that Midwest fishing-buffs dream about.

And since Michigan boasts hundreds of miles of Great Lakes shoreline and more than 2,886 miles of inland lakeshore (not to mention scores of rivers and streams), along with nearly 150 species of fish, it's especially important to get good advice about where the fish are biting.

So I sought out fishing pro Babe Winkelman, who, from his headquarters in central Minnesota, has carved out a fishing empire that includes books, videotapes, and one of the country's highest-rated syndicated television programs on the subject (*Babe Winkelman's Good Fishing*, check local listings for time and channel).

"The variety of fish that can be taken [in Michigan] is incredible," Winkelman said. "Just here alone, you have salmon, trout, steelhead, lake and brook trout, northern, muskie, walleye, crappie, sunfish, and more."

Winkelman knows all the top fishing holes. Here are three of his top Michigan picks:

- **Sturgeon Bay** "It can be hotter than a pistol in April," Winkelman said. "Mind-boggling perch fishing with fish up to 16 to 20 inches long. Fuzzy grubs and minnows are the bait to use. You're in a bay off Lake Michigan, so you can fish in small boats."

- **Little Bay de Noc** On Michigan's Upper Peninsula near Escanaba. "This is a great one and few people even know about it yet," Winkelman said. "There are small-mouth bass and big walleye. Also good fishing in Big Bay de Noc, and through this whole section of Michigan."

- **Tittabawassee River and Saginaw Bay** "It's usually incredibly hot in May (out in front of the river in the bay) for walleye that tip the scales at 13 to 17 pounds," Winkelman said. "By July, walleye fishing, very underrated, is better near the Charity Islands than on the rest of Lake Huron. The average guy can catch a bunch of big ones." This area is also renowned for perch and bass.

Of course, all the above "inside information" presupposes that you're an avid fishing fan who loves to angle regularly for big ones. But if you're just an occasional angler who'd still like a shot at big-time thrills, charter fishing might be just what you're looking for.

Coho salmon are the prize charter catch, and these lunkers can weigh in at more than 25 pounds. Actually, the abundance of the coho, introduced to the Great Lakes to feed on schools of small alewife fish, is a victory for both the conservationist and the recreationist. Today, cohos are the favorite target of Great Lakes anglers looking for a real fight. You hook one of these tigers on the end of your line, and you'll feel like Hemingway hooking a marlin out in the Atlantic. Well, sort of.

Among my favorite charter fishing paradises are Lake Michigan waters off South Haven and Saugatuck, strung along the eastern shoreline. Downtown harbor docks are lined with charter boats eager to take both dedicated landlubbers and seasoned pros out into the deep in search of trophy coho. All-day charters usually run $250 to $350; you can cut costs dramatically by splitting the fee with several friends. Half-day excursions also are available.

Finally, here are a few additional fishing facts that (I hope) will help your Michigan angling be more successful:

- If you've got *A River Runs Through It* fly-fishing fever, you should know that Gladwin County has more miles of trout streams than any other county in Michigan.

- St. Joseph's 1,000-foot-long North Pier is a good place for perch fishing from the shore.

- Fishing in Detroit? You bet. Belle Isle has at least three fishing hot spots: at the island's east end, on the south side (west of the Coast Guard station), and on the north side, across the channel from the Detroit Yacht Club. Your catch can include anything from silver bass and bluegill to salmon and pike. A bait shop is located about four blocks west of MacArthur Bridge, at 6220 East Jefferson. Besides offering worms and minnows, it can outfit casual anglers with fishing poles, line, and bobbers.

- Lansing's Riverfront Park and Trail boasts a noted fishing platform (at water level) that is always populated with anglers. What they're after is bags, walleye, steelhead, and coho.

- A special platform for handicapped anglers is located on the west bank of the Rogue River dam near Rockford, a popular fishing spot. Below the dam you'll find steelhead biting in the spring and salmon running in the fall. Above the dam, most plentiful are bass, pike, and panfish.

- Another perch-fishing hangout is South Pier in Grand Haven. Part of Grand Haven's two-mile-long boardwalk, it's also a good place to take in fabulous scenery.

- You would think that Fisherman's Island State Park, located south of Charlevoix, would boast great fishing. Actually, the biggest catch of this new and pristine state park is Petosky stones (shiny agates) found on the rugged shoreline.

Spring

FOR MORE INFORMATION

Contact Michigan Travel Bureau, P.O. Box 3393, Livonia, MI 48151, 800-543-2937. Ask for the booklet "Michigan Fishing and Specialty Charters."

9

Blooming Blossoms

BENTON HARBOR

IF IT'S OLD-FASHIONED FAMILY FUN YOU'RE AFTER, HEAD TO southwestern Michigan's dazzling annual Blossomtime Festival, an eight-day celebration of the state's "Fruit Belt" held in late April and flowering into May.

If the weather cooperates, you'll see hundreds of fruit orchard acres crowded with blossoms, heralding the much-anticipated arrival of strawberries, blueberries, peaches, and plums in this leading fruit-producing region.

And you won't want to miss the Grand Floral Parade, a fitting festival climax that is a spectacle of more than 110 colorful floats, marching bands, and exciting attractions. The giant parade alone draws 25,000 spectators.

The festival, more than a half-century old and one of the largest of its kind in the country, is held in the twin cities of St. Joseph and Benton Harbor. A product of hard work and cooperation by 30 area communities, it began in 1906 when local ministers urged fruit farmers to offer thanks for the region's generous harvests by blessing springtime fruit blossoms. Back then, ministers and residents would go out into the orchards to bless blossoming plants.

Some years ago, the ritual was moved indoors because of unpredictable and sometimes fierce spring weather. The ceremony can feature up to 10 priests, ministers, and other religious leaders, numerous choirs and musical groups, and residents from the tri-county farming region. It's an inspiring one-hour nondenominational service. Near the conclusion, blossomtime queens from the 30 surrounding communities present blossoming branches for blessing.

Of course, the real attractions are the blossoms. For about three weeks each spring, the region's countryside is a palette of pastel-hued fruit trees and bushes. Dainty pink apple blossoms, white cherry blossoms, yellow-blossomed blackberry bushes, and plum, apricot, and pear blossoms all paint the landscape breathtaking colors.

Specially designated Blossom Trails give you a chance to take a leisurely drive through fruit orchards at their peak of beauty; trails are pinpointed in festival programs available throughout the area.

Other highlights include:

- Blossomtime Carnival, with scores of carnival rides and games lining an old-time midway along Riverview Drive, providing excitement for kids and parents alike.

- Blossomtime Fashion Show, featuring the 30 community blossomtime queens modeling fashions from hometown stores in an annual fashion bazaar that attracts more than 1,000 people.

- Youth Parade, where more than 2,000 kids stroll down area streets displaying costumed family pets, decorated bikes, wagons, and homemade floats, while junior high school floats and marching bands compete to win a place in Saturday's grand parade.

- Wine tasting, boasting 15 of Michigan's wineries, along with Michigan cheeses, roast duck, and venison.

- Grand Floral Parade, a two-hour extravaganza witnessed by more than 25,000 people annually and featuring more than 100 units winding through the streets of Benton Harbor and St. Joseph.

- Races of 5k and 10k, and fun runs to benefit charity, are usually slated, with the racecourse beginning in Benton Harbor, following the St. Joseph River, crossing three bridges, and following the Grand Parade route to St. Joseph. Prizes for various age divisions are awarded; an entry fee is required.

- The Blossomtime Metric Century is the annual blossomtime bike tour offering pleasure rides of 15, 31, and 62 miles. Scenic routes wind along farms, woodlands, rivers, and orchards near Berrien Springs. Registration fee is required and includes tour route map, food stops, bike tour patch, caution flag, sag wagons (vans that hold repair kits and spare parts and pick up tired cyclists), and refreshments.

Now go out and smell the roses, or whatever else is blooming during blossomtime.

FOR MORE INFORMATION

Contact Southwestern Michigan Tourist Council, 2300 Pipestone, Benton Harbor, MI 49022, 616-925-6301.

10

Harbor Country

NEW BUFFALO

THE SUN LOOKED LIKE AN IRIDESCENT JEWEL AS IT WINKED brightly before slipping behind puffy white clouds. The clouds turned to mango pink as the sun disappeared from view, then changed to brilliant scarlet before the gold disk emerged again.

Yes, sunsets here in Harbor Country, miles of of sugar-sand shoreline stretching from Grand Beach to South Haven (and located just 75 minutes from downtown Chicago) are breathtakingly beautiful.

But there are lots of sunny delights in Harbor Country, old favorites mixed together with new enticements that make this summer place hugging the Lake Michigan shoreline the undisputed king of quick-trip weekend getaways from the city of big shoulders.

A great place to overnight is the Harbor Grand, a 57-room luxury hotel boasting harbor and lake views just off New Buffalo's main street. A long-needed alternative to the region's scores of bed-and-breakfast inns and summer cottages, the Harbor Grand is a classy grand dame that seems a perfect fit with the continued development along New Buffalo's marina district. It's also the only hotel on Lake Michigan between Chicago and South Haven.

Perhaps it's the hotel's Prairie School stylings, inspired by the architecture of Frank Lloyd Wright, that are responsible for its ambience of subdued elegance. Hardwoods gleam, and a handpainted mural over the lobby's grand staircase traces the region's history, which ranges from Native American crossroads to beachside resort town.

Guest rooms with harbor views feature gas fireplaces and whirlpools; ask for a second- or third-floor room on the harbor side to get all the above plus panoramic vistas of Lake Michigan. To compensate for lack of water views, rooms on the hotel's opposite side are all spacious two-room suites, perfect for kid-toting weekenders.

There's also an indoor swimming pool (which saved our rainy New Buffalo Sunday morning from being a disappointment for our kids) and a small fitness room that'll keep you in shape until you're back home at the health club.

The Harbor Grand's continental breakfast is surely a misnomer. A huge platter of fresh fruits (cantaloupe, watermelon, honeydew melon, blueberries, strawberries), fruit juices, and four different kinds of gourmet coffees please your morning palate. You can also choose among cold cereals and granola, as well as croissants, English muffins, and bagels. There are warm waffles, too. And don't pass up the most delicious chocolate-chocolate muffins, a sinfully delightful A.M. sweet-tooth treat.

Room rates are $105 to $150, including breakfast, through October. For more information and reservations, call 616-469-7700.

No one could ask for a better location. The Harbor Grand is just a block's stroll from both the increasingly trendy and upscale shops lining Whittaker Street, New Buffalo's main thoroughfare, and the town's magnificent beach.

A few boutiquing highlights:

My favorite remains Hearthwoods at Home, offering the likes of hand-peeled maple bunk beds, corner chairs, harvest tables, mirrors, and other furnishings fashioned by craftsman Andrew Brown from tree branches, cedar logs, and bark. The "urban primitive" stylings also rely heavily on "wood sense and tree karma," whatever that might be. But a browse around this studio is a must.

The Silver Crane, relocated from nearby Lakeside, has beautiful handcrafted sterling jewelry. Victoria's Attic boasts five rooms filled with works from 40 artists and craftspeople. We liked the French-type tapestries at The Villager.

And the Café at Michigan Thyme is a gourmet cook's delight. If you recently ran out of *pâté forestier au genievre* (pâté of pork, pork and chicken liver, mushrooms, and juniper berries), here's the place to restock.

Two other shops, the Climbing Monkey and Nancy Drew, provide endless splashes of artful fantasy and color; unique handicrafts, colorful paintings, and bric-a-brac can be found here in abundance.

Another one of Harbor Country's prime attractions is its excellent restaurants. Our newest discovery is Via Maria's at Brewster's, a tiny space made to resemble an ages-old Roman taverna. But it's the food that really excels, featuring handmade pastas (the spinach and cheese ravioli is delightful) and homemade breads. Especially enticing is the two-for $23.95 dinner deal, which includes salads, brick-oven-baked pizza with two toppings, and a pasta dish from the regular entrée menu.

Another newer downtown restaurant is Casey's Bar & Grill, an English-style pub that dishes out everything from calamari and tomato-pesto bread to grilled chicken tampico. Tony and Bruno's is a trendy and often crowded spot that reminds me of Bucktown's Club Lucky. And old favorites abound, like Miller's Country House, Red Arrow Roadhouse (100 different kinds of beer!), and Hannah's.

But regardless of where you eat, get yourself to the water. My girls love the New

Buffalo Beach, just at the end of Whittaker Street and adjacent to the harbor channel. Just sitting there is a pleasant way to pass a sunny afternoon, watching an endless flotilla of vessels, from kayaks and jet-skis to million-dollar yachts, move through the narrow inlet.

The beach itself is a great spot for families to enjoy some splashy fun in Lake Michigan. The gradually sloping sand allows you to go out almost half the length of a football field in just waist-high water. It's also a sand-castle builder's delight. There are two manned lifeguard towers, too. And my girls, ever the rockhounds, can pass an entire afternoon at the beach searching for oddly shaped and wildly colored stones that they later craft into their own "urban primitive" jewelry.

Behind the beach, tall sand dunes are etched with hiking trails up their backs. Climb to the top (or take the boardwalk) for vistas of an endless, mostly pristine shoreline.

Finally, the last "big new thing" might be Whittaker Woods, a championship 7,020-yard, par-72 golf course that opened July 4, 1996. Located on Wilson Road on the outskirts of New Buffalo, it might already be the best round of links in the region. Call 616-469-3400.

Other Harbor Country highlights:

Grand Beach   Chicago's Mayor Richard Daley has a family summer cottage in this quiet little village that traditionally drew the Windy City's South Side Irish Catholics to its environs. You can almost feel the tranquility as you pass through stately white gates leading to magnificent sandy beaches, sprawling green lawns, and tree-shaded streets. If you like what you see, overnight in the Tall Oaks Inn, formerly the Pinewood Lodge, where James Braddock trained for his heavyweight fight against Joe Louis in 1936.

Union Pier   I consider this tiny hamlet a refuge from the bustle of New Buffalo. You can rent a beach cottage by the week or month and call Lake Michigan's shoreline your own. Or overnight in one of the town's bed-and-breakfasts, which offer everything from Swedish fireplaces to rooms with lake views and whirlpools.

The town got its name from the now-gone Union Pier, built on Lake Michigan by lumbermen in the 1860s so that ships could carry cordwood and timber from surrounding forests to Chicago. It was quite an engineering feat for the mid-19th century, stretching 600 feet into the water and equipped with tracks so that mules and horses could pull timber from saw mills in the forests to waiting ships. Legend says those virgin forests were so thick "squirrels could run through the entire community without ever touching the ground."

Harbert   Its historic Swedish Bakery is my favorite Harbor Country sweet-tooth stop. Look for traditional Swedish breads, pastries, cookies, and cakes. Carl Sandburg once owned a goat farm near here; in fact, he wrote much of his Pulitzer Prize–winning work on Abraham Lincoln while living in these parts.

Warren Dunes State Park   Located between Harbert and Bridgman, Warren offers everything from beachy swims and mountains of sand to hiking trails and hang gliding. It's also the busiest state park, luring more than one million people annually from almost every state in the union. (So expect tremendous crowds on prime summer weekends.)

The two most popular dune climbs are Tower Hill (a favorite of kids and hang gliders) and Great Warren Dune, which offers a challenging trek to its 240-foot summit. You also can hike through Warren Woods, a 300-acre "forest primeval" that's never been disturbed by the saw.

Bridgman   This town boasts the Cook Nuclear Power Plant, which is one of the largest nuclear power plants in the

Harbor Country

United States. You can tour the plant (sort of) by visiting its next-door neighbor, the Indiana & Michigan Electric Company. Guided tours explain the plant's function, then show a film about the Cook plant, including the spot (about three miles out in Lake Michigan) where the plant's water is returned to the lake at least three degrees warmer than when it was collected.

St. Joseph   The city's downtown district is perched on a steep bluff overlooking Lake Michigan, near the spot where the French built Fort Miami in 1679. Besides historic turn-of-the-century homes and blossoming crab apple trees, it's noted for Silver Beach, a favorite spot of summer swimmers. It also has a 1,000-foot-long pier that leads out to lighthouses standing sentinel at the harbor's entrance; this remains a favorite spot for pier fishing throughout the year.

South Haven   A great summer resort town, South Haven boasts the closest thing to a California surfer beach that you'll find anywhere in the Midwest. North Beach, a miles-long sandy expanse fronting Lake Michigan, is crowded with string bikinis, muscled dudes, beach volleyball games, windsurfers, paddle ball gamers, joggers, sunbathers, swimmers—and there's still plenty of room for little kids who want to built sand castles in the surf.

It's also a major yachting and sportfishing port (most boats tie up at the mouth of the Black River), and there are plenty of lakeshore and riverfront shops for dedicated browsers to explore.

Other highlights include the Lake Michigan Maritime Museum; the historic Idler Riverboat, which has been transformed into a floating restaurant; Yelton Manor, an upscale Victorian-style bed-and-breakfast; July's annual Blueberry Festival that promises berry much fun (see Chapter 23); and Tree-Mendus Fruit Farm in nearby Eau Claire (see Chapter 30).

FOR MORE INFORMATION

Contact Harbor Country Chamber of Commerce, 3 West Buffalo Street, New Buffalo, MI 49117, 800-362-7251 or 616-469-5409; West Michigan Tourist Association, 136 East Fulton Street, Grand Rapids, MI 49503, 616-456-8557; Southwestern Michigan Tourist Council, 2300 Pipestone Road, Benton Harbor, MI 49002, 616-925-6301; Michigan Travel Bureau, PO Box 3393, Lansing, MI 48151, 800-543-2937.

Harbor Country

Summer

11

Island Odysseys

GREAT LAKES ISLANDS

MICHIGAN'S GREAT LAKES ISLANDS SIT LIKE JEWELS IN THE azure-colored waters that surround almost two-thirds of the state. Once the territory of missionary priests and French fur traders, and later ruled by English colonial powers, the islands are now a haven for vacationers, offering everything from grand hotels overlooking narrow straits to wolf-watching adventures in the wilderness.

If you're looking for the perfect island adventure for your weekend getaway, here are six of the top rocks to consider:

Isle Royale

With only 14,000 visitors annually, Isle Royale is the country's least-visited national park in the lower 48 states. It is also one of the most fascinating—a rugged, remote retreat shaped by glaciers more than 12,000 years ago. It remains a spectacular pristine wilderness, complete with its own 14-member wolf pack, 34 varieties of wild orchids, and the country's largest moose herd outside Alaska.

It takes a 50-mile, six-hour ferry ride from Copper Harbor or Houghton to get to Isle Royale, which rests in the wild waters of Lake Superior; boats run mid-May through September. The island, stretching 45 miles long and 9 miles wide, is a backpacker's paradise, boasting 165 miles of trails that even the most casual trekker will find relatively easy. Its 42 inland lakes filled with lake trout, walleye, and northern pike should satisfy any angler. If you'd rather opt for a canoe adventure (or desire a fishing guide), these can be found at Rock Harbor Lodge, the island's only hotel.

Besides hiking, camping, nature photography, and stalking the stately moose (the island herd numbers about 1,400), another good way to see the island starts aboard the lodge's MV *Sandy*. The boat swings out into the bracing air of Lake Superior to give you a water view of the wilderness isle, then docks to begin a leisurely guided trek to island landmarks.

Most visitors glimpse a moose or two during their visit. Wolves are seldom seen and generally stay far away from humans—though you might get lucky and hear them baying at the moon.

Grand Island

Grand Island National Recreation Area, located about one mile offshore in Lake Superior (just north of Munising), is one of the most recently designated nature preserves in the United States. The primitive wilderness rock, about seven miles long and four miles wide (about the size of Manhattan), is a naturalist's paradise, with dramatic sandstone cliffs rimming the island and soaring more than 300 feet above the pounding waves. You might spot a pair of bald eagles who call the island home, along with a few sometimes frisky black bears, white-tailed deer, ruffed grouse, red squirrels—and a pair of professors who live in a lighthouse that's

900 feet above sea level, said to be at a higher elevation than any other in the world.

Hiking the wilderness isle is extremely satisfying, but can be difficult and sometimes downright hazardous. There are no paved roads among its 13,500 acres of forest. Trails are rough, some leading close to conifer swamps, and there are only two designated campsites (on Murray's Bay and Trout Bay) that have toilet facilities. Pitch your tent anywhere else on the island and you're back in the days of the French voyageurs who once roamed these shores.

Beaver Island

Beaver Island, located 18 miles from the nearest coast, was once the site of the mainland United States' only declared monarchy—or so the story goes. That's because this Lake Michigan rock was home to one of the state's most notorious historic figures.

In 1848, James Jesse Strang, a self-declared successor to Mormon Church founder Joseph Smith, brought his followers to this remote outpost. Less than 10 years later, more than 2,500 Mormons lived on the island, causing the original Irish immigrant fishermen who settled here to flee.

At first Strang participated in mainstream politics, winning himself a seat in the Michigan senate. But soon the charismatic leader made a bigger grab for power, declaring himself king over the island's (willing) inhabitants and "breaking away" from the rest of the United States.

This so-called kingdom didn't last too long. In fact, some say it was Strang's decree that women always wear bloomers that sparked a revolt among the people, resulting in Strang's death. All that's left today of his legacy is the Mormon Print Shop and Museum, which explains his reign.

Today, about 400 people live on the island year-round. It's long been a center for northern Lake Michigan's fishing industry, but that's dropped off dramatically due to over-fishing, an encroaching alewife population, and pollution. What remains is a pleasant isle, reached only by a two-and-a-half-hour ferryboat ride from Charlevoix, that revels in its isolation from the pressures of the outside world. If you visit here, be prepared to relax.

North Manitou

It's said that North Manitou's 15,000 acres of wilderness is a reminder of what most of Michigan must have been like before the fury of the lumbermen's saws. Located in Lake Michigan, just west of Leland, the primitive island's many inland lakes make it an angler's paradise. It also boasts a hearty flock of wild turkey and lots of deer, a challenge for hikers in the summer and hunters during the harvest season. Especially noteworthy are the "Ten Commandments," a group of 10 virgin white birch trees that are beautiful to behold, and an elm so massive that, visitors say, it takes five people, "finger-to-finger," to span its girth.

South Manitou

It's ironic that this is the more-visited island of the two, because in centuries past Native Americans considered it so sacred they almost never used it. (They believed the great spirit, Manitou, lived here.)

Like its twin, South Manitou is a remnant of the great glaciers that once scoured the earth, leaving debris that resulted in these landforms. Besides great hiking trails that crisscross the island, and abandoned, centuries-old farms, the island has two main attractions: you can tour its 125-year-old lighthouse that's perched on the rocky shore, and visit the Valley of the Giants, a stand of virgin white cedar trees, one of which is the all-American champ at 111 feet high.

Mackinac Island

The Grand Hotel, one of the few remaining great hotels of the railroad and Great Lakes steamer era, stands sentinel over the Straits of Mackinac, which separates Lakes Michigan and Huron. Built in 1887, the hotel's many-columned 660-foot veranda, positioned on a high bluff overlooking the straits, provides magnificent vistas of the surrounding waters (a fee is charged).

It's just one of many spectacular attractions on this island, a summer paradise for Midwesterners. And its turn-of-the-century ambience is heightened by the island's ban on motor vehicles. Get your walking shoes on, rent a bicycle, or hire a horse-drawn buggy to sightsee the rock.

Among its highlights:

• Fort Mackinac, a 19th-century British-built fort used to defend the straits against those upstart colonists during the Revolutionary War, features musket firing demonstrations, guided tours of restored fort buildings—even a court martial reenactment on the fort's central parade grounds.

- Hub of downtown's activity is the ferryboat docks, which receive travelers to the island from mainland Mackinaw City and St. Ignace, and downtown shops that carry everything from souvenir gewgaws to fudge.

- Walk along the island's boardwalk for magnificent sunset vistas.

- Historic architecture is everywhere. Two of my favorites: Haan's 1830 Inn, a bed-and-breakfast situated in a stately Greek Revival house onced owned by the fort's physician, Col. William Preston; and St. Anne's Church, whose congregation began worship here in 1695, making it one of the first churches in the region.

- Rent a bike and cycle along the road that circles the island; it's an eight-mile pedal. Along the way, sight-seeing highlights include beautiful lakeshore scenery and craggy rock formations like Sugar Loaf, a 75-foot-tall pinnacle at the island's center, and Arch Rock, a natural land bridge considered holy by Native Americans.

For More Information

Contact Beaver Island Chamber of Commerce, Box 5, St. James, Beaver Island, MI 49782, 616-448-2505; Superintendent, Isle Royale National Park, Houghton, MI 49931, 906-482-0984; Mackinac Island Chamber of Commerce, Box 451, Mackinac Island, MI 49757, 906-847-3783 or 800-454-5227; Michigan Department of Natural Resources, State Parks Division, P.O. Box 30228, Lansing, MI 48909, 517-373-1270.

Summer

12

Aboard a Fightin' Sub

MUSKEGON

"DIVE! DIVE! DIVE!" COMES THE VOICE OVER THE SHIP'S speaker.

I can feel the sub slant downward into the black sea, silently feeling its way toward its prey. We are after supply ships, tankers, all kinds of cargo boats. Now the captain's voice sounds throughout the vessel.

"Officers to the war room!"

"Up periscope!"

The captain peers through the looking glass.

"Steady now. Torpedo room ready?"

"Aye, aye, Captain."

"Stand by to fire number one torpedo."

"Standing by to fire torpedo number one."

"Fire number one!"

He doesn't take his eye off the scope for what seems an eternity. Suddenly he lets out a loud breath.

"Good work, men," he says. "A direct hit. That's one less tanker Uncle Sam will have to worry about."

Of course, this is a generic scene from countless World War II movies I saw on the "Late, Late Show" when I was a kid. John Wayne, Robert Mitchum, Kirk Douglas, Clark Gable: it seems all the Hollywood legends commanded submarines on the big screen.

And those famous movie scenes are what flooded my memory when I stepped onto the USS *Silversides*, an authentic World War II submarine berthed at Muskegon Lake, just east of Heritage Landing and west of downtown Muskegon.

This is the United States' most celebrated submarine. It sank 23 Japanese ships (more than 90,000 tons) and hit 15 others while on 14 patrols in Pacific waters after setting sail following the disaster at Pearl Harbor. It was so successful at infiltrating enemy waters that during one reconnaissance mission, it's said, crew members even watched a Japanese horse race by periscope.

While on tour you'll learn that the *Silversides* accommodated eight officers and 72 men; once you see the cramped quarters, claustrophobic from bow to stern, you'll be amazed that more sailors didn't crack up while on patrol. After all, submariners were on these ships for 45 consecutive days before getting any time off.

Tours take visitors to the fore and aft (front and back) torpedo rooms, engine rooms, battery, bridge, and control room. Everything looks as if it were frozen in time during the war; in fact, those are the same brass torpedo doors, cables, dials, gauges, sonar controls, radios, and charting tables that the sub used during the conflict. It is so well preserved that it looks as if it could set out to sea on a moment's notice.

While this is a fascinating historical artifact of ocean warfare, let's pray that our country will never again have to use submarines for anything other than maneuvers, training missions, and Navy base open houses.

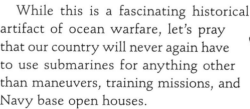

Summer

For More Information

The USS *Silversides* is located at 740 West Western Avenue. Tours are offered April through mid-October; you can arrange for special tours during other parts of the year. Admission is charged. Contact USS *Silversides*, Muskegon, MI 49443, 616-755-1230; or Muskegon County CVB, P.O. Box 1087, Muskegon, MI 49443, 800-235-3866.

Aboard a Fightin' Sub

13

Michigan for Free

SO YOU'RE WORKING ON A SHOESTRING HOUSEHOLD BUDGET. You've already started squirreling away dollars for the Christmas season. Or maybe you're just plain fed up with paying hefty Disney World–level admission fees for tourist attractions.

Cheer up! You can still enjoy a weekend ramble to some of Michigan's top museums, historical sites, architectural wonders, and wacky establishments—without paying a penny. Here's a look at a half-dozen of Michigan's best freebies.

Custer Capers

If you're a George Armstrong Custer fan, head to Monroe's County Historical Museum. Custer grew up in this hamlet (founded in 1790, nestled on the shores of Lake Erie) and visited friends and family during breaks in the Civil War, where he first achieved fame as the conflict's youngest general, at age 23.

The little museum, which attracts worldwide attention for its Custer memorabilia, is the home of the general's campaign sword, rifles, photographs, and other artifacts. One of the most interesting remnants is his buffalo robe, worn during the 1868 Washita Wars when he conducted raids (some say unnecessarily brutal) on the Sioux. To get some sense of the petite size of the infamous soldier, note how small the robe is. Open year-round. Call 734-243-7137.

Peaceful Reflection

For me, one of Michigan's most inspiring attractions is the Cross in the Woods, located at 7078 State 68 (off 1-75) in Indian River. The peaceful landscaped grounds feature the world's largest crucifix, standing in a clearing surrounded by tall pine trees. The 55-foot-tall crucifix was carved from a single redwood tree and weighs 14 tons; it bears a 7-ton statue of Christ. The complex also includes an out-door church, carillon, shrines, and an interesting nun-doll museum. Open April through November. Call 616-238-8973.

The Big Dipper

Kitch-iti-kipi (the Big Spring) at Palms Book State Park, 12 miles west of Manistique, is one of the Upper Peninsula's most popular natural attractions. Visitors hop aboard a float-ing observation raft, pull themselves by a rope system across the spring waters, and view the wonders contained in the crystal-clear waters.

The Big Spring is 45 feet deep and 200 feet across, its water temperature a constant 45 degrees year-round. The spring boasts all kinds of fish and strange rock formations—not to mention more than 16,000 gallons of water bubbling up from the depths.

While this remains a favorite U.P. spot for me, it's also where I received one of the biggest "thrills" of my life. As my raft tour settled in the middle of the spring, someone on board started getting all excited about spotting a school of large fish. Almost everyone ran to that side of the little raft, nearly capsizing it. I had visions of the *Titanic* as my brother and I clung to the opposite side of the raft in hopes of avoiding an impromptu trip to Davy Jones's locker. We did. The park's open year-round; rafts operate in mild weather. Call 906-341-5010.

Fascinating Fishies

If you think there's something fishy at the Wolf Lake Hatchery, located about 10 miles west of Kalamazoo, you're right. Millions of fish are "grown" annually at this facility, with huge aquarium tanks holding vast flotillas of chinook salmon, brown trout, muskie, sturgeon, and northern pike. Other visitor center highlights include a history of Great Lakes fishing, a 47-pound catfish, and a plaque commemorating the state's record catch of a 193-pound lake sturgeon. See if you can spot the three monster sturgeon lurking in the murky waters of the hatchery's outdoor ponds. One measures nearly six feet long and is more than 50 years old. Kids (and adults, too) get a kick out of feeding steelhead trout, which also swim in these ponds. Open year-round. Call 616-668-2696.

Holocaust Memorial

On a much more serious note, visitors to the Holocaust Memorial Center in West Bloomfield Township (suburban

Detroit) are offered a chilling experience with exhibits detailing the atrocities committed by Nazi Germany during World War II; as many as six million Jews, along with Gypsies and other victims, were murdered in cold blood as part of the Nazis' hideous "Final Solution."

Self-guided tours of the $7 million museum begin benignly enough with the sounds of Jewish lullabies sung by a mother to her children. But soon visitors walk through a darkened tunnel of increasing horror: films of a ranting Adolf Hitler exhorting a swelling Nazi throng, displays of Holocaust victim artifacts, photos, and gut-wrenching dioramas depicting the savagery. (Many of the displays may be too graphic for children under 13.)

Guided tours are offered Sunday afternoons. The museum is located at 6620 West Maple in West Bloomfield Township, two miles west of Orchard Lake Road, in the Jewish Community Center across from Henry Ford Hospital. Open year-round. Call 313-661-0840.

For More Information

Contact Michigan's Upper Peninsula Travel & Recreation Association, P.O. Box 400, 618 South Stephenson Street, Iron Mountain, MI 49801, 906-774-5480; West Michigan Tourist Association, 136 East Fulton Street, Grand Rapids, MI 49503, 616-456-8557; Michigan Travel Bureau, P.O. Box 3393, Livonia, MI 48151, 800-543-2937.

14

Mackinac Island Escape

MY YOUNGER DAUGHTER, DAYNE, WOKE UP FROM A DEEP
sleep with rapid-fire travel questions for her papa.

"Are we going to Mackinac Island today?"

Yes, I said.

"Are we going on a boat?"

Yep.

"A motorboat?"

Well, yes.

"Will it go fast?"

Uh-huh.

"I'll throw up."

She didn't, but Mackinac Island is always an adventure
anyway—especially when you take two little girls on the
1,000-mile round-trip car tour from Chicago to the Straits of
Mackinac, a narrow channel of water that both connects
Lakes Huron and Michigan and separates Michigan's upper
and lower peninsulas.

Once sacred ground to Chippewa Indians, home to
rugged French fur traders, and object of battles between British and American soldiers, Mackinac Island today is a haven
of Victorian charms. Nearly 800,000 visitors a year are lured
to its brightly colored turn-of-the-century buildings, horse-
drawn carriages, bluff-top British frontier fort—and possibly

more fudge shops per square acre than anywhere else in the world.

For three days, my wife, Debbie, and I gave daughters Kate and Dayne, ages six and four, carte blanche to create a kids' dream vacation on the island. Their blueprint for fun, one that anyone can duplicate, included an eight-mile round-the-island bike tour (on State 185, the nation's only state road where autos are prohibited), frequent fudge-shop detours, and dancing till midnight at a rock-and-roll bar in our hotel.

Now for the details.

Bitter weather at the start of our early-summer island sojourn required that the kids don winter hats and coats for the ferry crossing from Mackinaw City. Wind howled and rain blew like a North Sea gale as temperatures dipped to a frosty 38 degrees, but the Arnold Transit line's catamaran "jet boat" whisked us to the rock in only 16 minutes.

A 10-minute walk up the island's east shore brought us to our digs at Mission Point Resort. Mission Point is an ideal family hotel, boasting special kid programs like storytelling, sunset hayrides, a game-filled activity center, nighttime Disney movies, and the "Kids' Club," a daily three-hour afternoon get-together with supervised arts, crafts, games, and sports.

It may also have the most good-natured, kid-friendly staff on the island. On more than one occasion, our kids had hostesses, waitresses, and even the concierge participating in "step-on-the-flowers-only" rug games in the dining room hallway while we finished breakfast.

Even our room rated squeals of approval from Kate and Dayne; it offered panoramic views of Lake Huron and an opportunity for endless sightings of "those neat white seagulls."

The kids were eager to hit the road, so we rented bicycles. Debbie and Kate shared a tandem, while I chauffeured

Dayne in the child's seat of my bike. (Hourly and daily rates are available for regular bikes and tandems.) This is easily the best method to visit island hot spots, eliminating lots of whining about walking. For example:

Kate: "You expect me to walk from HERE all the way to THERE? No way!"

Dayne: "If you make me take another step, I'll fall on the ground right on my face."

No motor vehicles are allowed on the island, so horses are everywhere, something that delighted our animal-loving kids. Though Kate, who's already planning to be a veterinarian, was devastated to learn that you must be at least eight years old to solo-ride a livery horse through town. You can also rent a horse and carriage to get around. "Cowboy" experience is not necessary; these nags know the roads better than any visitor.

We opted for a 90-minute guided carriage tour, which originates downtown near the ferryboat docks. It took us down historic Market Street (home to some of the island's oldest houses, including that of fur baron John Jacob Astor); up the hill past the Grand Hotel (which charges a fee to walk along its 660-foot veranda); and to Arch Rock, a prehistoric "natural bridge" reaching 150 feet above the water while spanning 50 feet across it.

Another big kid hit was Fort Mackinac, built in 1780 by the British to protect their fur empire against those upstart Americans. Perched high on a bluff overlooking the town and straits, the military outpost is loaded with family fun.

A "must-visit" is the Children's Discovery Room, housed in the Officers' Stone Quarters, one of Michigan's oldest buildings, with four-foot-thick walls to withstand anticipated American naval attacks from the harbor. The hands-on haven includes push buttons that elicit "sounds of history," like firing muskets, marching soldiers, and clopping

Mackinac Island Escape

horses and buggies; and an exhibit imploring kids to "reach into the past," where they can touch beaver hats, sword handles, and flintlock pistols.

Best is the uniform room, where kids dress in 1880-style blue army uniforms, complete with brass buttons and pointy helmets, and pose for pictures behind a lieutenant's desk.

Other fort highlights include guided tours led by costumed soldiers, musket and cannon firings, and a court martial played out on the parade grounds. Don't miss a chance for a welcome rest, cold beverage, and spectacular water vistas at the fort's Tea Room, which clings to the side of a high bluff.

Kate and Dayne also gave high marks to walks along West Bluff (just west of the Grand Hotel) and East Bluff (east of Fort Mackinac), areas renowned for splendid turn-of-the-century summer homes sporting the best of Victorian architecture. And you can't find better spots to view breathtaking sunsets than the island boardwalk, just west of downtown on State 185, or Fort Holmes, located in the island's interior.

Eventually the kids found a place to ride horses by themselves, hopping aboard Thunder and Buckshot at Chambers Riding Stable, Market Street and Cadotte Avenue. The horses, tethered to an exercise wheel, walk in a circle, but they might as well have been galloping over unbroken prairie judging from the smiles on the girls' faces.

"I never want to leave Mackinac Island," said Kate.

And they each developed a dreamy crush on a rock-and-roll singer at Mission Point's Round Island bar. Each evening from 8:00 P.M. to midnight he belted out classic rock tunes on his synthesizer with mostly little kids crowding the dance floor while their parents sat close by, seemingly content to observe the action.

Our girls literally danced until they dropped, lasting until 11:20 the first night, then closing down the joint the next evening. The singer thrilled Dayne by dancing with her once, then had Kate swooning as he knelt alongside her while crooning a ballad.

When we got back to our room, Kate's comment pretty much summed up our Mackinac visit: "I knew this island thing was going to be SO great."

FOR MORE INFORMATION

Mission Point Resort offers daily room rates and lodging packages; for reservations and information, call 800-833-7711. For Fort Mackinac information, call 906-847-3328. Mackinac Island is about 400 miles north of Chicago. For more island tourism information, contact Mackinac Island Chamber of Commerce, P.O. Box 451, Mackinac Island, MI 49757, 906-847-3783 or 800-454-5227.

Mackinac Island Escape

15

Steaming Across the Great Lakes

LUDINGTON

AT THE HEIGHT OF GREAT LAKES' CRUISING HISTORY, MORE than a half-dozen ferryboats regularly crossed Lake Michigan carrying passengers, cars, trucks, and freight between Michigan and Wisconsin.

Now there's only one left.

The newly refurbished SS *Badger*, a 410-foot-long steel-hulled ferry steamer, sails between Ludington and Manitowoc, Wisconsin, from May through October. Believe me, it's the closest thing to long-distance ocean cruising you'll find in the Midwest.

Built in Sturgeon Bay, Wisconsin, and launched in 1952, the *Badger* can hold 600 passengers, 120 automobiles, and a crew of 60. In its peak years, the *Badger* and its sister ship, the *Spartan* (no longer operating), transported 153,000 passengers, 132,000 railroad freight cars, and 54,000 automobiles annually.

It's an eight-hour round-trip between ports, and many weekenders simply ride the waves from one side to another for sheer "cruise ship" excitement. You can walk the decks while taking in swelling waves, listen to squawking gulls, marvel at views of long Great Lakes freighters, soak up the sun in a deck chair, or relax in a weather-protected observation room.

There's a breakfast buffet served in the ship's Upper Deck Café. Fresh fruit, scrambled eggs, sausage, ham, hash browns—even French toast sticks, scalloped apples, and sausage gravy with biscuits—are part of the menu. At the Badger Galley, lunch and dinner treats include modest selections like homemade pizza, soups, salads, and sandwiches. Or just grab a cold brew and enjoy the ride while the kids spend their quarters in the ship's video arcade.

When travelers from Ludington arrive at Manitowoc, they'll undoubtedly have a few hours' layover before the ship heads back to Michigan. Fortunately, there are more than a few pleasant diversions.

Summer

In keeping with the theme of your cruise getaway, head to the Manitowoc Maritime Museum, a $2 million state-of-the-art museum featuring a fascinating collection of Great Lakes maritime artifacts, shipbuilding displays, and regional history. But the museum's main claim to fame is the USS *Cobia*, a World War II submarine (sitting adjacent to the museum) and designated National Historic Landmark.

It's similar to the 28 U.S. Navy subs built in Manitowoc during the war. But the *Cobia*, which saw combat action in the Pacific, retains most of its wartime fittings. So when you hear the "Dive! Dive! Dive!" command broadcast over the ship's loudspeaker, you'll get an idea of what it was like to skipper this deadly ship. In fact, guided tours take you through the entire sub, from the claustrophobic quarters of bunks and mess rooms to the control room, where you can even look through the sub's periscope, scanning the waters of Lake Michigan.

Also check out Manitowoc's Rahr-West Art Museum, housed in an 1891 Victorian mansion that contains a collection of 19th- and 20th-century American paintings, including one by Georgia O'Keeffe.

Just outside of town, the Pine-
crest Historical Village features 23
restored buildings, including three
150-year-old log cabins. Nearby
Two Rivers ("Trivers," as locals
call it) offers the Rogers Street Historic Fishing Village, with an 1866 three-

masted schooner, the *Buddy-O* fishing tug, a shipwreck
museum filled with recovered artifacts, and an 1886 lighthouse that once stood at this village's harbor entrance.

For an even more romantic trip across the lake, enjoy the
Badger's newest wrinkle—it's also a kind of floating bed-and-
breakfast. During selected dates (generally from the last
week in August through mid-October), you can overnight
dockside in a stateroom that has two single beds, a sink, a
lavatory, and a window overlooking the water. Room rates
do not include regular passenger and vehicle fares.

If you do decide to cruise on the *Badger*, you'll be in good
company. The rich and famous who've traveled on this historic Great Lakes ship include everyone from Jack Benny and
Tammy Wynette to The Who and Weird Al Yankovich.

Weird Al?

For More Information

Contact Lake Michigan Carferry, P.O. Box 708, Ludington,
MI 49431, 800-841-4243; Manitowoc Lakeshore Develop-
ment and Visitors Bureau, P.O. Box 903, 1515 Memorial
Drive, Manitowoc, WI 54221, 800-262-7892; Ludington
Convention and Visitors Bureau, 5827 West U.S. 10, P.O. Box
160, Ludington, MI 49431, 800-542-4600.

Steaming Across the Great Lakes

16

Saugatuck Idyll

BOTH MY DAUGHTERS RATE SAUGATUCK AS A FAVORITE Michigan weekend treat. They like to shop (an inherited gene from their mother), swim in Lake Michigan, and explore nearby sand dunes.

Come to think of it, I like to do all that stuff, too!

Located on a channel of the Kalamazoo River with mountainous dunes and Lake Michigan a stone's throw away, this quaint hideaway has been luring visitors to its small-town charms for more than 100 years. It's a haven for Chicago weekenders. In fact, locals will tell you that it is not unusual for folks to get off nearby I-196 for a "rest stop" one weekend and be back to buy property the next.

Saugatuck was founded in 1824 by William Butler, a genuine Connecticut Yankee. Bypassed by the railroads, it retains the charm of a quaint New England coastal village, bedecked with sailboat masts, tall shade trees, and quaint white clapboard homes (many of which are becoming year-round residences rather than weekend retreats).

To start your Saugatuck ramble, head to its bustling downtown district. In season, "bustling" may not be quite the right word; "gridlocked" might be a better one. But you're here to enjoy and relax, so what's the rush? Here you'll find an eclectic mix of upscale shops offering everything from ship's bells to designer clothes. It's impossible not to stop inside Saugatuck Drugs on Butler and Mason, belly up to its old-fashioned soda fountain, and order a thick chocolate shake. Of the village's many art galleries—Saugatuck is one of the Midwest's oldest art colonies—the Joyce Petter Gallery remains my favorite. Besides a lively mix of American painters, the gallery features interesting architectural touches (old columns, gates, etc.) and a courtyard that often showcases special collections.

The kids also like to release some of their always-present high energy at downtown's Wicks Park on Water Street at Main. Here they swing on swings, teeter-totter, and run themselves ragged. One of our most treasured family vacation pictures has the entire clan hanging from the monkey bars; that includes grandma and grandpa, too.

For water thrills, head to Oval Beach just west of town on Lake Michigan. You can get there from downtown Saugatuck by taking the historic chain ferry across the Kalamazoo River (admission charged, operates Memorial Day through Labor Day), running from Mary and Water Streets to Ferry Street. Prepare for crowds at the beach; this is the favorite spot in Saugatuck for splashy thrills. You can rent giant inner tubes and cabanas, and there are changing rooms and a snack bar.

While at the beach, try your hand (or should I say, "foot") at climbing Mt. Baldhead, a 260-foot-plus sand dune that's said to be the tallest in the region. You'll be rewarded with great views of Saugatuck, nearby Douglas, and Lake Michigan.

Speaking of Douglas, its long stretches of white-sand beach are my kids' favorite spot for water thrills. Some of our best times in this area were spent building sand castles, diving into the lake's white-water waves, and burying each other in the sand.

Of course, if you'd prefer to ride over the dunes instead of just look at them, hop aboard one of the souped-up buggies offered by the Saugatuck Dune Rides, which operates daily May through September, and October weekends. The "buggies" are actually converted three-quarter-ton Dodge pickups that roar up and down the sandy slopes while the jokester driver yells things like, "Look out! We're headed into the water!" So be prepared for great scenery and lots of yuks.

Sightseers also have plenty to do in Saugatuck. Tour the ss *Keewatin*, a restored turn-of-the-century passenger steamer of the Canadian Pacific Railroad. Located just south of the Saugatuck-Douglas bridge, it has been maintained as an "in-service ship," with many of its elegant original furnishings, such as hand-carved mahogany interiors, luxurious staterooms, and an Edwardian dining room.

Or get onto the water during narrated cruises offered by the *Queen of Saugatuck*, a re-created stern-wheel paddleboat that plies the waters of the Kalamazoo River and Lake Michigan. Called "one of the very best Lake Michigan boat rides," the 67-foot, 80-plus-passenger ship has guides that explain both Great Lakes sailing lore and local geography. For example, you'll learn that the shoreline here has eroded several hundred feet in the past 100 years. (Board at the Fish Dock on Water Street.)

Overnighters are fortunate that Saugatuck offers more country inns and bed-and-breakfasts than any other little town in the state. Among the choices are the Park House, built in 1857 and retaining its Greek Revival simplicity and country-home decor; the Rosemont Inn (in Douglas), with a front porch that overlooks Lake Michigan; the Wickwood Inn, elegantly decorated with Laura Ashley wallpapers and antique and reproduction furnishings, and featuring a sunken garden room and screened porch; the Kemah Guest House, formerly the home of a sea captain, with touches of Frank

Lloyd Wright and Art Deco; Twin Gables Country Inn, an 1865 treasure with pressed-tin ceilings and timbers cut from the historic Singapore sawmill; and downtown's Maplewood Hotel, where new suites include whirlpool baths.

FOR MORE INFORMATION

Saugatuck celebrates several summer arts festivals. For festival dates and more information, contact Saugatuck-Douglas Visitors Bureau, P.O. Box 28, Saugatuck, MI 49453, 616-857-1701.

Summer

17

Exploring Shipwreck Treasures

YOU WON'T FIND THE KIND OF TREASURE TROVE MEL FISCHER did when he discovered the lost gold ship *Atocha* off the Florida Keys. But Michigan has five underwater bottomland preserves that contain many shipwreck treasures revealing the Great Lakes history. The unique preserves are some of the Midwest's most inviting, though slightly waterlogged, spectacles.

"Michigan has more than 38,000 square miles of Great Lakes bottomlands," said John Halsey, chief archaeologist for the state's Bureau of History. "Over the years lots of ships, beginning with LaSalle's *Griffin* in 1679, have come to grief in one way or another." The turbulent Great Lakes' waters contain an "enormous concentration of wooden and metal wrecks that number more than 3,000," Halsey said. "Those kinds of numbers are unmatched anywhere in the world."

Many of the ships were lost in the last quarter of the 19th century. Ships hauling timber and ore often were cut down from schooners and side-wheel steamers already 50 years old, so it didn't take much before they gave up the ghost in rough weather.

What makes diving these shipwrecks so exciting is that many of them remain excellently preserved and "have been that way in some cases for 150 years," according to Halsey. He explained that the Great Lakes' cold fresh water acts as a preservative even for the oldest wooden ships, which would be consumed by destructive animal life in warm salt water. "Salt water is a kind of chemical soup," Halsey said. "Within a matter of years, wrecks in that environment could be gone."

As for sunken treasure, salvaging is illegal, but all that divers are likely to find is cargo like copper ingots, iron bars, and the like. "Some early-day steamers carrying immigrant families westward from New England went down with the life savings and possessions of those people," Halsey said. "But even in the 1840s and 1850s, hardhat divers were searching those wrecks for money, gold, and other objects."

One of the bonuses of these bottomland preserves is that "all five protected areas hold some type of shallow wreck accessible even to beginning divers," said Mike Kohut, an expert diver who offers beginner classes in underwater diving techniques through his Recreational Diving shop in Royal Oak. (For preserve diving you must be scuba certified; adult education classes are taught at most YMCAs.)

Of the five protected bottomlands, Alger Underwater Preserve, located on the south shore of Lake Superior near Munising, is a beginner's paradise, Kohut said. One wreck, the *Bermuda*, sits almost intact in 20 feet of water. Visibility (30 feet at a depth of 100 feet) is also considered to be among the best in the Midwest. Other wrecks include the *Dreadnaught*, an 1880s ship intact in 25 feet of protected water and a photographer's delight; the *Manhattan*, a wooden-hulled freighter that sank in 1903 in 40 feet of water; and the *Superior*, a steamer that foundered off Picture Rocks in 1856—the oldest known wreck in the preserve.

In Thunder Bay Underwater Preserve, in Lake Huron between South Point and Middle Island, the 550-foot freighter *Nordmeer* sits in water so shallow that parts of the wreck (including the center deck) are above water and can be seen from shore.

Roaring winds, pounding seas, and foggy mists caused many shipwrecks in Lake Huron's main shipping channel, now home to the Thumb Area Bottomland Preserve. However, many of the near-virgin wrecks lie in extremely deep water (some of them more than 120 feet down with poor visibility). It's the same at Lake Superior's Whitefish Point Underwater Preserve, with several intact wrecks more than 150 feet down.

While the Straits of Mackinac Preserve contains many relics of Davy Jones's locker, they're accessible mainly to experienced or expert divers. The two premier wrecks are the *Cedarville*, a 700-foot ore carrier sunk in 1966 that lies totally intact in 100 feet of water; and the *Sandusky*, a wooden schooner that went down in 1856 and now stands upright and intact at 80 feet. "It's probably the nicest wreck in the lakes," Kohut said.

Archaeologist Halsey reminds divers that it is essential to keep wrecks as intact as possible. "To allow salvaging on these wrecks is probably the most wasteful thing," Halsey said. "The preserves are trying to maintain shipwrecks as long-term recreational, historical, and archaeological resources. "But self-policing of the diving community is the only way we'll save them. They're easy pickings for people who do not embrace the preservation ethic."

For More Information

Charter operators rent diving equipment at most sites; average cost is about $50 per day. For dive-tour information, contact Recreational Diving, 4424 North Woodward, Royal Oak, MI 48073, 800-999-0303; for more information about Michigan's bottomland preserves, call 800-543-2937 and ask for that brochure.

Exploring Shipwreck Treasures

18

In the Navy

MICHIGAN PORTS

NOW HEAR THIS.

If you'd like to tour one of the Navy's finest warships, walk its decks, visit the war room, and maybe even marvel at its massive gas turbine engines, get permission to come aboard a fully decked-out fightin' frigate dropping anchor at a seaport near you this summer.

A sleek, gray, guided-missile frigate sails the Great Lakes and weighs anchor at Midwest port cities (including several in Michigan) every summer as part of the Navy's annual Great Lakes Cruise, first launched in 1959 with the opening of the St. Lawrence Seaway.

Of course, the magnificent warship is a great recruiting device, luring sailor wannabes with its hulking presence, technological wizardry, and opportunities to sail the world. It also gives the Navy a chance to debunk the standard myth going around that the Navy's not hiring because of much-publicized base closings and decommissioning of ships. In fact, the Navy needs to recruit between 60,000 and 90,000 people each year just to replace those who are retiring or completing their tours of duty.

But the ship's appearance also gives tens of thousands of Midwesterners each year a chance to walk aboard an honest-to-goodness warship that looks like it came out of a special-effects lab of a Hollywood movie studio.

It's also a great opportunity to see up close what you're paying for with your tax dollars!

Generally, Navy frigates stretch about 450 feet from bow to stern (that's a little more than the length of one and a half football fields), weighing in at 4,100 tons with a full load. They're deadly, too. Frigates are equipped with Harpoon and Standard Missiles, a 76 mm/62 caliber gun, and six torpedo tubes. And they can cut through the waves at more than 30 knots (about 34 MPH).

Tours generally start amidships. You'll learn a little history about guided-missile frigates, a new class of destroyer that numbers more than 50 ships—the Navy's largest "new fleet" since World War II. They're designed to ensure quick-reaction defense against surprise antiship missile attacks, providing protection for military and merchant shipping, among other uses.

Highlight of the tour might be the ship's combat information center, a darkened room behind the bridge that contains all kinds of radars, weapons-control systems, and technological gewgaws—state-of-the-art defensive systems that might put Star Wars gadgets to shame. For example, three digital computers offer immediate evaluation of potential threats detected by the ship's radars, digital sonars, and other shipboard sensors.

The frigate's response to hostile actions can include anything from surface-to-air and surface-to-surface missiles to antisubmarine warfare torpedos.

It is not to be messed with!

You'll also tour the bridge and signal bridge (where the flags are flown) and take up-close peeks at the ship's torpedo tubes. And, depending on the ship's sched-

Summer

ule, you might get to tour its engine room. The engines are truly a sight to see: two massive, computer-controlled General Electric LM2500 gas turbines generating 40,000 horsepower. (These are engines similar to those found in a DC-10 commercial jetliner.)

Let's not forget the crew. Visitors can chat with sailors and share their experiences of being on a modern naval warship. Corny as it might sound, you can't help walking away from one of the these warships feeling proud to be an American.

Tours are free, offered on a first-come, first-served basis. Be sure to call ahead for more information and to double-check port schedules.

FOR MORE INFORMATION

Michigan ports of call usually include Sault Ste. Marie, MI, 313-259-1004; Muskegon, MI, 313-259-1004; and St. Ignace, MI, 800-821-1670. Or call Public Affairs at Great Lakes Training Center for a full schedule, 847-688-2024.

In the Navy

19

The Forgotten Coast

PORT HURON TO BAY CITY

WITH ITS MILES OF MOUNTAINOUS SAND DUNES, SPECIALLY
designated national lakeshore, sleepy beach and resort
towns, and ever-present Hemingway legacy, western Michigan seems to get all the attention.

But what about the forgotten coast, that stretch of shoreline along eastern Michigan's "thumb" that edges Lake
Huron, offers all kinds of historic gingerbread houses, and
boasts the best sunrises in the state?

Here are some of the highlights:

The lakeshore road that outlines the "thumb" covers some
of the state's most spectacular scenery, passing through
sleepy harbor villages offering charming bed-and-breakfasts,
charter fishing adventures, and quaint shops. Port Huron is
one of Michigan's oldest towns, the site of the 1686 French
Fort St. Joseph, which was charged with keeping the British
out of the Great Lakes. It presents interesting little shops, a
"boardwalk" along the Black River, and other riverfront vistas where you can watch giant freighters pass through the
St. Clair River channel linking Lakes Huron and Erie.

Tour the Fort Gratiot Light, America's oldest lighthouse
in continual operation; the 86-foot-tall light tower has been
guiding ships around rocky shoals since 1825. In Pinegrove

Park, you can see the retired lightship *Huron*, a 97-foot-long floating lighthouse whose beam could be seen by ships more than 15 miles out at sea. The Museum of Arts and History there includes eerie artifacts recovered from local shipwrecks.

That museum also offers memorabilia from Thomas Edison's boyhood home. Edison grew up here and as a teenager sold newspapers and magazines on trains between his hometown and Detroit to earn money for experiments, which he conducted in the train's baggage car. This arrangement ended when he accidentally set fire to the car; he was fired, too.

Then there's the Blue Water Bridge, a structure I consider almost the eighth wonder of the world. The one-and-a-half-mile-long bridge rises 152 feet above the St. Clair River to allow massive modern freighters and ore ships to pass underneath.

While Port Huron celebrates a festival or two during the year, nothing compares to the three-day Port Huron to Mackinac Island Yacht Race, held in July. Count on everything from carnival rides and live entertainment to a grand fireworks display.

Lexington, located about 20 miles north of Port Huron, is a pleasant little town filled with Victorian architecture and boutiques, but its claim to fame is fruit pies. Stop at Mary's Pie Shop for a taste of these delicious treats. Or head to Lexington's Croswell Berry Farm, renowned for its black raspberry, cherry, and red raspberry pies.

Continuing north, you reach historic Port Sanilac on Lake Huron, which has more than 40 buildings over 100 years old. In addition to a few ship captains' mansions converted into charming bed-and-breakfasts, the village has the Sanilac Historical Museum, housed in an 1872 Italianate mansion with an eclectic collection of everything from pioneer log cabins and Indian pipes to a dairy museum.

Summer

The next town of note, Port Hope, is famous as the jumping-off point for the Thumb Area Bottomland Preserve (see Chapter 17). This is a protected shipwreck preserve open to all scuba divers—who should know that it is illegal to remove any artifacts from sunken vessels.

Port Austin, located at the tip of the "thumb," celebrates both sunrise-watching over Lake Huron and sunset-watching across Saginaw Bay. Its fishing-village ambience is perfect for tours of historic buildings, especially those at the Huron City Museum. Here nine restored buildings dating between 1850 and 1890 include the 1881 House of the Seven Gables, the Phelps Memorial Church, and the Point Aux Barques United States Life Saving Station.

Other activities can include visits to the Austin Reef lighthouses; canoe trips on the Pinnebog River; tours of the now-closed Grindstone City quarries; and the Sanilac Petroglyphs, a series of sketchy images carved into stone by prehistoric people. One of Port Austin's "shouldn't miss" destinations is Port Crescent State Park, a wonderland of duneland shores and beachcombing delights.

Finally, you'll reach Bay City, a port that owes its existence to the Saginaw River, which once floated logs through town to lumber mills bordering the stream. As a result, many of the city's prime attractions remain on or near the river.

The city is noted for its tree-shaded streets, many lined with Victorian and Georgian mansions (especially on Center Street) built by 19th-century lumber barons. A good place to start your tour is the City Hall and Bell Tower, an 1895 Romanesque building that has been meticulously restored. Inside the council chamber, there's a 31-foot-long tapestry woven by Polish artist Monika Chmielewska that depicts village history. If you're willing to climb stairs to the Bell Tower, you'll be rewarded with sweeping vistas of the city, Saginaw Bay, and its waterways.

The Forgotten Coast

Maybe you'd like to hop aboard the *Bay City Belle*, a 49-passenger stern-wheel riverboat docked in Wenonah Park that offers cruises on the Saginaw River from May through mid-October. Or just stroll the two-and-a-half-mile-long Riverwalk, which hugs the Saginaw's west bank and offers views of all kinds of sailing craft and oceangoing freighters.

For more natural beauty, visit Jennison Nature Center, part of Bay City State Park, located about five miles north of town on State 247. Hiking trails lead trekkers on a tour of the area's unique ecological characteristics. Then head to Tobico Marsh on Killarney Beach Road, 1,700 acres of the largest remaining wetland on Saginaw Bay's western shore. Climb a 30-foot tall observation tower for panoramic views of the marshy landscape; it's an especially good vantage point during spring and fall waterfowl migrations.

If you want to see Bay City at its wildest, visit during the Fourth of July Festival. The bash draws more than 600,000 people to the tiny town, mostly for fireworks displays so huge it takes three days to shoot off the colorful blasts.

Summer

FOR MORE INFORMATION

Contact the Port Huron Chamber of Commerce, 810-985-7101; Bay Area CVB, 901 Saginaw Street, Bay City, MI 48708, 517-893-1222 or 800-424-5114; St. Clair County Convention and Visitors Bureau, 800-852-4242; Michigan Travel Bureau, P.O. Box 3393, Livonia, MI 48151, 800-543-2937.

20

Mining Legacies

HANCOCK, CASPIAN,
IRON MOUNTAIN

FOR CENTURIES BEFORE EUROPEANS ARRIVED, NATIVE Americans mined rich copper deposits found in the Upper Peninsula, especially on or near the Keweenaw Peninsula. But because it took heavy mining machinery and lots of industrial muscle to uncover the state's almost pure iron deposits, they weren't excavated until the 1870s.

And then, how Michigan's mining business boomed! Beginning with the discovery of iron near Negaunee in 1844, the iron industry has dug up nearly $50 billion worth of iron ore. Add $10 million from Keweenaw's copper deposits. Then compare it with California's gold boom, which adds up to only about $10 billion to date. So Michigan's gritty mining riches are more than five times greater than those harvested in California, where the glittery gold rush grabbed all the attention of history books.

That's pretty darn impressive. So are the museums, mines, and massive equipment left over from the heyday of Michigan's mining boom. If you'd like to dig up the scoop on these mining legacies, here are the best places to go.

Iron Mining

Start at the Michigan Iron Industry Museum on Forge Road, about three miles east of Negaunee. It's nestled on Carp Creek, where the state's first iron forge operated. Through mining artifacts, photographic displays, and an enlightening slide presentation, you'll learn how one modest iron mine grew into a string of 40 that produced more than one million tons of iron annually.

Of course, iron is not a renewable resource, so once these deposits were exhausted in the 1870s, mining companies moved on to other parts of the U.P.—like the Gegobic Range west of here.

You'll also learn that none of the Upper Peninsula's mines are producing ore these days. In fact, the best they can do is taconite pellets, a product made by processing poor deposits of ore into iron pellets only 65 percent pure. The pellets are then shipped to foundries around the Great Lakes. Open daily, May through October; admission is free. Call 906-475-7857.

At the Iron Mountain Iron Mine, located on U.S. 2 about nine miles east of Iron Mountain, you'll descend more than 400 feet beneath the earth to pass through more than a half-mile of underground tunnels and drifts.

First don your hard hat and raincoat, given to all visitors before they enter the sometimes drippy mining shaft. The 35-minute guided tours lead you through lighted caverns for close-up views of spectacular rock formations; you'll ride the same railway system that took miners to their dirty jobs until the mine closed in 1945. You'll watch experts operate huge mining machinery, including drilling machines that seem to reach eardrum-bursting levels of sound after only a few minutes of demonstration. Imagine listening to that noise eight to ten hours each day.

You'll also marvel at "puny" antique mining equipment and wonder how miners of the 1870s ever dug out these mountains of iron ore. It was a gloomy, difficult, dirty, noisy, dangerous job, taking three men digging with pick and shovel more than 10 hours to advance four feet. Oh yes, the highest-paid employee was the blaster, who set explosives inside these claustrophobic tunnels. He earned 25 cents per hour. Open June through mid-October; admission is charged. Call 906-563-8077.

Iron Mountain's Chapin Mine, discovered in 1879, was one of the wettest iron mines ever worked in these parts or anywhere else in the world. At the height of its operation, it took a crew of 60 men to operate the massive 725-ton pump that sucked water out of deep mine shafts. Some statistics are startling. The flywheel of the pump is 40 feet in diameter and weighs 160 tons. It averaged 10 revolutions per minute, pumping out about five million gallons of water daily. The engine's high-pressure cylinder has a 50-inch bore, and the low-pressure cylinder is 100 inches in diameter. The stroke of the pistons is 10 feet. Yes, it is a monster. Open Memorial Day through October; admission is charged. Call 906-774-1086.

Copper Mining

At Coppertown USA in Calumet, you'll learn that the landscape of the Keweenaw Peninsula is dotted with hundreds of historic mine shafts, buildings, and rock piles that tell a tale of the quest for copper ore. Artifacts, photographs, and other exhibits explain that Michigan's copper industry actually began thousands of years ago when ancient Native American miners chipped away with sharpened stones and other crude tools at exposed veins of pure copper.

You'll also learn that the U.P. was the site of America's first great mineral rush, beating out California's famed gold stampede. But the region's last copper mine closed in 1968.

Now rock hounds, not miners, explore old diggings to uncover slivers of pure copper left in the ground. Open June through September; admission is charged. Call 906-337-4579.

You'll see the world's largest mine hoist at the Quincy Mine Hoist, located on U.S. 41, one mile north of Hancock. This behemoth, technically named the Nordberg Hoist, has been called one of the wonders of the mining world; it's listed on the National Register of Historic Places.

The steam-powered hoist, which weighs nearly two million tons, is located near the Quincy Mine Number Two Shaft House. It hauled 10 tons of copper ore at a speed of 3,200 feet per minute, or 36 MPH, from a record maximum depth of 9,260 feet—that's almost two miles underground. Though no longer operable, it's an amazing sight to see. After all, it mined more than one billion pounds of copper from 1856 through the 1930s.

Other attractions include two narrow (three-foot) gauge locomotives used to handle copper ore here from 1890 through 1945. Guided tours also reveal that only 10 percent of all copper ore from the mine has ever been harvested, but the depth at which the copper is found here makes it uneconomical to operate (at least in these times). Open June through Labor Day; admission is charged. Call 906-482-3101.

You'll be plunged more than a quarter-mile into the depths of the earth during tours of the Arcadian Copper Mine, located on State 26 about one mile east of Hancock. You travel through underground labyrinths of mine shafts where the temperature remains a year-round 40 degrees. At the mine's information center, you'll learn more about this industry that gave this part of the Upper Peninsula its nickname—Copper Country. You'll also see copper and agate specimens in the mine's lobby shop. Open June through mid-October; admission is charged. Call 906-482-7502.

Another chance to examine the miners' working conditions awaits you at Delaware Copper Mine, off U.S. 41 near Copper Harbor. The 40-minute tours take you nearly 125 feet down into the mine's main shaft, which operated from 1847 to 1887. On the first 10 levels of this mine, miners removed more than 3,500 tons of copper. You'll also see remnants of prehistoric copper mining pits and historic 19th-century mine company buildings. Open May through October; admission is charged. Call 906-289-4688.

FOR MORE INFORMATION

Contact Michigan's Upper Peninsula Travel & Recreation Association, P.O. Box 400, Iron Mountain, MI 49801, 906-774-5480.

Mining Legacies

21

Bavarian Blast

FRANKENMUTH

IMAGINE PAT BOONE SINGING "DEUTSCHLAND UBER ALLES" while dressed in lederhosen and white buck shoes.

Okay, so the squeaky-clean entertainer didn't warble in leather shorts during his visit to "Michigan's Little Bavaria." But his all-American act, along with German-style architecture, parades, beer gardens, wiener schnitzel, and a healthy dose of gemütlichkeit (friendliness), drew more than 350,000 people just a few years ago to the annual Frankenmuth Bavarian Festival, held in mid-June.

That's not surprising, though. The eight-day bash in this hospitable hamlet always draws overflow crowds to celebrate its cultural heritage, which started in 1845 when 15 Lutheran missionaries from Germany settled along the Cass River and established a tidy little community that was much like their Bavarian homeland.

These original settlers brought with them classic Bavarian skills, such as woodcarving, sausage-making, milling, and brewing hops and barley malts into strong dark beer gulped from foot-high steins—and the community thrived. Even after the turn of the century, German remained the town's principal language. Today its ethnic roots are showcased in a rash of Bavarian extravagance stretching from one end of

Main Street to the other, where more than 100 shops and restaurants captivate visitors.

And does Frankenmuth get visitors—more than three million people every year descend on this little bit of Europe (town population is around 4,500) to browse among the shops, gaze at Old World architecture, and celebrate at the Bavarian Festival.

The Bavarian Festival, headquartered at Heritage Park in downtown Frankenmuth, is the town's ultimate open-armed *willkommen* to all. The real action begins with the Bavarian Festival Parade. More than 120,000 people each year enjoy decorated floats, marching bands, giant helium-filled balloons depicting fairy tale characters, and ethnic dancers.

"Wurst Day at the Fest" presents dinnertime samples of more than 25 delicious sausages made by Frankenmuth's own, served with sauerkraut, boiled potatoes, baked beans, and homemade bread in an all-you-can-eat extravaganza. Entertainment is provided by a German oompah band. Advance tickets are available to this popular event; the price includes general fest admission and food.

Big-name concerts also are slated during the fest. Dinner show tickets (baked chicken, smoked pork chops, dressing, gravy, and music) are available, but they must be purchased 72 hours before the performance.

And the Youth Parade is a miniature version of the big blast featuring hundreds of youngsters who've made their own floats and costumes.

Other fest highlights:

- The Children's Grove boasts a petting zoo with all kinds of lovable creatures; twice-a-day circuses with live small-animal acts; the *kinderhaus*, where volunteers help kids glitter, paste, and create art surprises; and a magic workshop.

- *Sommer Garten* food stands offer barbecue chicken dinners along with traditional German treats like bratwurst and sauerkraut; roast beef sandwiches on *kummel weck* (caraway seed buns); stollen (fruit bread), pastries, and cookies; and refreshing steins of locally brewed Frankenmuth Brewery Pilsner and Old German Dark. Also count on costumed Maypole dancers, musicians, comics, and pony rides.

- The Marketplace is where you can stroll among woodcarvers, silversmiths, clockmakers, and other craftspeople at work.

- The Dance Tent, resembling a Munich *biergarten*, features nonstop toe tapping to Bavarian and polka dance bands plus German spirits.

There's lots more to see outside the festival grounds. Frankenmuth might be best known as the home of Bronner's Christmas Wonderland, the planet's largest Christmas store. Year-round displays contain more than 50,000 ornaments, lights, and decorations. Nativity scenes range from thumbnail-small to life-size. And there are more than 250 fabulously decorated Christmas trees dotting the aisles. I dare you to leave without buying something.

The town claims two restaurants that are counted among the 10 largest in the United States. The cavern-size Bavarian Inn and Zehnder's (both located on Main Street) are nationally noted for their all-you-can-eat, family-style chicken dinners. You also can count on hearty German dishes like wiener schnitzel, sauerbraten, and Bavarian dumplings.

Residents became so enamored of early American covered bridges that they built one of their own. The Holz-Brucke is a 239-foot-long, 19th-century-style covered bridge spanning the Cass River; it connects the above-mentioned restaurants.

Don't miss the 35-bell carillon imported from Germany at the Bavarian Inn's Glockenspiel Tower. Large crowds always gather at noted hours to hear three melodies and see animated figures reenacting the legend of the Pied Piper of Hamelin.

And be sure to see the St. Lorenz Church, one of the town's most recognized landmarks, built in Gothic splendor in 1880 with stained glass windows portraying Frankenmuth's history and a 167-foot-high steeple.

Free shuttle buses from the festival grounds to these attractions are available; passenger pick-up points are marked with signs. Another free bus tour takes you to a working farm for a firsthand look at Michigan agriculture; check for dates. Or you can hop aboard guided motorcoach city tours that start at the Fischer Platz behind the Bavarian Inn; admission is charged.

Finally, visit Frankenmuth Brewery, Michigan's only suds factory, which makes Old German–style beers. Tours are Monday through Saturday, 10:00 A.M. to 6:00 P.M., and Sunday, noon to 5:00 P.M. (It's located at 425 South Main Street.)

For More Information

There is a charge for fest admission. Contact Frankenmuth Convention & Visitors Bureau, 635 South Main Street, Frankenmuth, MI 48734, 517-652-6106 or 800-386-8696.

22

Pleasure Island

LITTLE BLACK LAKE

HERE'S A SPLASHY WAY TO BEAT THE DOG DAYS OF AUGUST'S simmering, sun-drenched heat. Head to Pleasure Island, where you can challenge "Michigan's longest waterslide" or dare to dive into the chuming waters of the "Black Hole."

Thrill seekers or nondaredevils just hoping to soak up the sun's rays will love this little waterpark, located near Hoffmaster State Park, midway between Muskegon and Grand Haven. It's built around four shallow lagoons that offer everything from waterslides to bumper boats and includes a sandy beach on the shore of Little Black Lake.

Of course, most people come to Pleasure Island for splashy thrills. The waterpark is renowned in the Midwest for the "Black Hole," a five-story waterslide that drops you through a green translucent tube twisting and turning *inside* a hill and deposits you with a whoosh into a pond of water. Believe me, it's kind of spooky in there.

Another crowd pleaser is the "Rampage Water Coaster," a four-story tower that speeds riders down a 45-degree-angle slide. At the bottom, you skim across the water for up to 200 feet.

The Runaway River, reputed to be Michigan's longest waterslide, provides cool thrills. So does the "Twister," my daughter Kate's favorite: two corkscrew slides that twist and turn at a leisurely pace down five stories of chutes and flumes, ending in a gentle shallow-water splash. Then there's "Thunder Falls," which captures the thrills of tubing over a waterfall. Yes, you read that correctly: over a waterfall.

One of the most distinctive features of Pleasure Island is that all waterslides end in pools of water less than two feet deep. That means you don't really have to know how to swim to enjoy most of the fun. And parents of little ones can rest easier knowing that kids are just a quick grab away. Of course, free life jackets are available for young ones and non-swimmers, if that's what it'll take for mom and dad to be more comfortable with the watery surroundings.

There are also kiddie slides far less challenging than the monster drops. And water cannons and trolley drops. Or families can lounge on the tranquil "Lazy River" inner tube float, then relax on the park's sandy beach.

Finally, here are a few tips to help you enjoy your water-park visit:

- Bring two sets of car keys, since they're the most commonly lost items at waterparks.

- Don't forget beach towels, sunglasses, sunscreen (at least number 15), and footwear.

- Get to the park about 15 minutes before opening so you'll have a choice of parking spots.

- Stake a claim to lounge chairs or areas nearest to the activities you enjoy most.

- Do not leave money or credit cards unattended. Buy a sealable "neck safe" container on a string that hangs around your neck. Leave the bulk of your valuables back in your hotel safe.

- Arrive at the park's opening or after 4:30 P.M. to avoid peak crowds. Weekends can be especially frustrating, with long waits in long lines for most activities.

- When it does get crowded, head to rides with shorter lines, like lazy rivers and kiddie play areas.

- Peak crowd period is a good time to have lunch or browse gift shops.

Now, let's get wet.

For More Information

Pleasure Island is open Memorial Day weekend through Labor Day. Contact the park at 99 East Pontaluna Road, Muskegon, MI 49444, 616-798-7857.

Pleasure Island

23

Blueberry Bash

SOUTH HAVEN

I WAS SURPRISED TO DISCOVER THAT MICHIGAN BOASTS THE largest area of blueberry cultivation in the world, with an annual yield of nearly 55 million pounds. In fact, it even claims a "blueberry belt," a wedge of cultivated blueberry fields stretching along the eastern shore of Lake Michigan from Ludington to Michigan City.

So you can count on plenty of juicy blueberries during the state's midsummer blueberry harvests, when scores of U-pick farms offer blueberries that can be added to spice up almost any treat. But if you're really blueberry-crazy, head to South Haven's annual mid-July National Blueberry Festival, celebrated in the heart of southwestern Michigan's blueberry belt.

As king of this festive, five-day, family fun bash, the blueberry is prominent in parades, concerts, and other entertainment. But you also can participate in windsurfing races, sand-castle-building contests, a perch fishing tournament—more than 50 events in all. It all translates into the biggest "party" celebrated around these parts.

Fest fun usually begins with a downtown kids' parade, where homemade blueberry costumes seem to bring the succulent fruit to life. There's also a farmers' market and blueberry bash concert, which add to the excitement.

However, it's the pie-eating contest (which takes place outside City Hall on Phoenix Street in the downtown district) that's clearly the festival highlight. Anyone can enter to eat mounds of blueberry pies in this timed event, which is divided into several age groups. But remember: rules call for contestants to eat without using their hands at all. Be assured of seeing a mess of blue-stained faces.

Another winner is the outdoor kick-off concert along the river; advance and at-the-gate tickets are available. The "Blueberry Dessert," a kind of "Taste of . . . ," showcases all manner of blueberry goodies and other foods. Other weekend activities usually include a pancake breakfast, an antique auto show, a craft fair, bicycle tours, and more.

Make sure you head over to the giant blueberry balloon; that's where you pick up buses for tours of blueberry farms, where you'll be able to pick your own berries.

If you want a break from berry-mania, I'd suggest a stroll along South Haven's more than five miles of white-sand beaches. Especially fun is expansive North Beach, the most "California" beach I know in the Midwest. You'll see everyone from muscled dudes to string-bikinied dudettes strolling the sand. There are volleyball games galore on the shore, and plenty of space for little tykes to build sand castles by the waves.

FOR MORE INFORMATION

Contact Greater South Haven Chamber of Commerce, 535 Quaker Street, South Haven, MI 49090, 616-637-5171. For a list of U-pick farms, contact Southwestern Michigan Tourist Council, 2300 Pipestone, Benton Harbor, MI 49022, 616-925-6301.

24

Sleeping Bear Dunes

GLEN HAVEN

IF YOU THINK CLIMBING A 150-FOOT SAND DUNE WOULD BE A blast, have I got a place for you: the ever-changing world of shifting sands at Sleeping Bear Dunes National Lakeshore in Glen Haven. It's the Great Lakes' most famous dune-packed shoreline and stretches for almost 35 scenic miles along the waters of Lake Michigan.

The sprawling national preserve on the northwestern corner of Michigan's lower peninsula draws more than a million visitors every year to its sandy shores, where mounds of migrating dunes extend more than two miles inland. It takes its name from a Chippewa legend about a mother bear and her two cubs, separated and stranded in the lake by a raging forest fire. Mother bear climbed a bluff (now marked by a solitary dune) in a futile vigil for her offspring; the two nearby Manitou Islands represent her lost cubs.

In this hilly preserve, fringed by walls of coastal sand dunes and 300-foot bluffs, dotted with clear inland lakes and rimmed by Lake Michigan, you can hike or drive to scenic overlooks and history-rich museums. Or just perch atop a hillock and admire the wonderful world of the Sleeping Bear.

Start by learning a little bit of dune history at the visitors center (located just outside the village of Empire); displays, slide shows, and a brief movie explain the story of these sandy hills.

One of the interesting dune facts you'll discover is that major geological changes usually take millions of years, while Sleeping Bear can change dramatically within decades. Twice this century, massive landslides at Sleeping Bear Point have shifted dune landscapes and buried trees under new mountains of sand. In fact, the restored U.S. Coast Guard station at Glen Haven had to be moved from Sleeping Bear Point in 1931 because of the threat from migrating dunes.

The visitors center also offers information about 12 hiking trails that meander through the dune community; hardcore trekkers can even purchase topographical maps to plan their wanderings.

Perhaps the easiest way to experience the dunes is by puttering along the seven-and-a-half-mile Pierce Stocking Scenic Drive (main drive entrance is located about two miles north of Empire, on State 109). Dune overlooks include a view of the shoreline down to Empire Bluffs and, less than a mile away, a peek at a large vanishing dune being swept away by strong winds.

If you're a hiker, one of the best routes is the Empire Bluff Trail, a one-and-a-half-mile round-trip self-guided walking tour taking you to a Lake Michigan overlook that offers maybe the best vista of the entire Sleeping Bear shoreline. Halfway to the lake, the trail becomes quite steep, until you reach high lakeshore bluffs. You might even discover hang gliders here, since it's a favorite launching site for sky-fly daredevils.

Long-distance hikers can try the Platte Plains Trail, a 15-mile stretch that includes trail loops along streams, through cedar swamps, and past streams diverted by huge beaver dams.

Of course, the most popular trail at Sleeping Bear is the Dune Climb, a tough, nearly three-mile-long, 150-foot-high ascent of this mountain of sand (go all the way to the top for a breathtaking overlook of Lake Michigan). This live sand dune, once rising 600 feet above the water, is migrating due to shifting sands, wind, and wave action; its front portion is actually sliding into Lake Michigan. This is a tough climb, especially in summer when the sand is hot and temperatures are unforgiving. Use plenty of sunblock, bring water, wear a hat—and take your time.

If you'd rather be beaching, Good Harbor Bay (at the park's northernmost point) offers miles of white-sand beaches, an undeveloped site, and great views of Pyramid Point bluffs and North Manitou Island. Empire's village beach is more civilized, with picnic areas, grills, playgrounds, and rest rooms.

One of my favorite historic spots in the dunes is the Sleeping Bear Point Coast Guard Station Maritime Museum, a half-mile west of Glen Haven village. The white clapboard station house, built in 1901, serves as the museum's focal point. It ceased its ship-in-distress rescue operations in 1994, after plucking many a survivor out of the Manitou Passage, a deep but narrow shortcut that claimed hundreds of ships.

The handsome building, on its beautiful lakefront setting, houses exhibits on Great Lakes shipping, cargo, and history, with photos depicting the activity-filled schedule and rescue techniques of these brave men. There's even an eerie shipwreck display with recovered wreckage: doors, life jackets, and other artifacts. Upstairs is the seven-man bunkroom for the service crew, restored to its early 1900s look. It's hard to imagine seven people sleeping in these cramped quarters, let alone storing all their gear in little closets the size of a tiny attic crawlspace.

The village of Glen Haven is on the National Register of Historic Places. Though most buildings are

Sleeping Bear Dunes

currently boarded up awaiting funding for National Parks restoration, its architecture and layout offer a terrific example of a company town at the turn of the century, when the region was the domain of lumbermen and merchant sailors. Sleeping Bear Inn, built in 1860, shows just what a fine frontier hotel looked like.

If you feel even more adventurous, take a 90-minute ferry ride out of Leland (located on the northeastern point of Good Harbor Bay) to South Manitou Island, a historic rock pile that once bustled with supply stores provisioning Great Lakes shipping steamers that anchored in the island's then-busy harbor.

Today, the peaceful island is an out-of-the-way wilderness paradise. Sign up for a one-and-a-half-hour guided tour of the island to see artifacts of its storied past. Highlights include the South Manitou Lighthouse, built in 1871 to guide ships through the treacherous Manitou Passage (the wreckage of the freighter *Francisco Morazon* is just off South Manitou's south shore); more sand dunes; a gull colony on the island's eastern shoreline; and the Valley of the Giants, with its world-record virgin white cedar trees, some of which measure nearly 18 feet around.

FOR MORE INFORMATION

Contact Sleeping Bear Dunes National Lakeshore, National Park Service, 9922 Front Street, Empire, MI 49630, 616-326-5134. Ferries leave downtown Leland May through September; for rates and schedules, call Manitou Island Transit, 616-256-9061 or 616-271-4217.

25

Lock Around the Clock

SAULT STE. MARIE

As we crossed the three-mile-long International Bridge leading from Michigan's Upper Peninsula into Canada, we stopped at the Customs Officer's booth to answer typical who/what/why questions.

"Are you all citizens of the United States?" he asked, eyeballing myself, my brother Mark, and daughters Kate and Dayne.

"Uh-huh," I answered.

"Any liquor or firearms in your possession?"

"Nope."

"And what's your purpose for coming into Canada today?"

"Actually, for dinner," I said.

The officer looked kind of stunned. "You're coming into Canada to eat dinner? That's a new one." But after a few more serious looks into the car, he waved us through, and there we were, in the Great White North searching for food.

It's not that the U.P. ran out of burgers during our recent ramble to the Soo Locks area. It's just that the girls wanted to visit Canada again (we've been there on some trip five years in a row), and I wanted to eat at Giovanni's, one of many good pasta restaurants in this heavily Italian city. Kate and Dayne also wanted to sample their favorite Canadian fast food—Tim Horton's Donuts, an ex–hockey player's franchise that seems to be on every street corner in every Canadian province.

Of course, we'd really made the trip this far north to visit the world-famous Soo Locks, which rest on the St. Mary's River between Sault Ste. Marie, Michigan, and the like-named, larger Canadian city across the border.

The locks form a passage for deep-draft tankers and freighters around the rapids in the river, which is the only water connection between Lake Superior and the other Great Lakes. They're also the world's biggest and busiest locks system, averaging more than 12,000 vessels each year. The size of these ships varies from small passenger boats and working vessels to huge cargo ships carrying more than 72,000 tons of freight.

A good place to start a tour of the locks, operated by the U.S. Army Corps of Engineers, is the Visitors Center on Portage Avenue. Not only does it contain photographs of the locks' construction, but it boasts a scale model of how the locks work when ships approach them, along with other informative displays.

But perhaps the center's most important function for visitors is the daily schedule board telling which freighters are due to arrive at the locks within the next few hours. So though we headed to the elevated viewing platform for a birds-eye view of a few ships passing through the locks, we noted a special treat slated for late that night: the *Paul R. Tregurtha*, a 1,041-foot-long monster of a freighter that's the largest ship plying Great Lakes' waters, would be arriving just before midnight.

That gave us some time to wander the town, especially Portage Avenue and its cacophony of souvenir, marine, and fudge shops, which have sprung up to take advantage of the immense popularity of ship-watching across the street.

To experience the total package, head to the Great Lakes Shipwreck Historical Society store. While listening to Celine Dion's hit from *Titanic*, "My Heart Will Go On," we browsed among marine artifacts such as diving helmets, instrument markers, and a rescue squad canoe in a neat display; lighthouse collections; model cargo ships (going for $1,500!); guidebooks to diving Ontario shipwrecks; scrimshaw ($5,000!); and plenty of memorabilia about the most famous Great Lakes shipwreck, the *Edmund Fitzgerald*. Of course, the girls most like *Titanic*-mania-inspired White Star Line hats and T-shirts.

After more sight-seeing and dinner in Canada, we headed back to our hotel (the Ojibway, an elegant little hotel right across the street from the locks) for a swim. Then we returned to the viewing platform at about 11:30 P.M. to wait for the monster cargo ship to arrive.

It almost looked like a low-flying UFO, lit up by a string of bright lights, when we first spotted it approaching the locks. And it seemed almost as big as the mother ship of *Independence Day* when it got to the locks gate.

Of the four locks here, only the Poe Lock is big enough to handle the *Tregurtha*. Built in 1968, the Poe is 1,200 feet long, 110 feet wide, and 32 feet deep. The *Tregurtha* literally squeezed into the space.

It was pretty amazing to watch the massive ship rise in front of our eyes like some impossible David Copperfield illusion. In just a few minutes, the locks chamber raised the hulking ship 21 feet from Lake Huron's water level to Lake Superior's water level.

We waved to the sailors on board; they waved back. And we watched as the Great Lakes' largest ship passed into the black night, its lights soon disappearing into the dark haze. In the end, the vast waters remain as mysterious as ever.

Of course, there are other ways to see the Soo Locks. One is the sailors' way—actually riding through them. Climb aboard one of the Soo Locks Boat Tours to experience the locks with freighters and other ocean vessels.

The two-hour, rain or shine international boat float takes you through the locks, where your boat will be raised 21 feet straight up to the level of Lake Superior. You'll also get a surrealistic, close-up view of Canada's massive Algoma Steel plant, complete with blast furnaces firing and 10,000 employees scurrying. It looks like something right out of a futuristic Bruce Willis movie. And you'll glimpse Ontario's Sault Ste. Marie, more than five times larger than its American counterpart. See if you can spot planes swooping into the city's seaplane station, where they load—on the fly—water tanks for dousing forest fires. Boat tour fare is $14 for adults, with kid and senior rates available. Call 800-432-6301 or 906-632-6301.

Or hop aboard the Soo Locks Tour Trains, another two-hour journey. The narrated tram tour climbs 135 feet above the gigantic locks system on the three-mile-long International Bridge. From up there, you can see 10 miles down the river and take great photos of one Canadian and all four American locks.

The train also passes directly above St. Mary's Rapids, where you'll hear the roar of the water as it crosses into Canada. There you'll visit the historic Old Stone House; Queenstown, lined with shops; North America's tallest self-supporting cross; the Algoma Steel plant; and more. You can even stop for additional shopping and dinner and return on a later train if you'd like. Cost is $11 for adults, with rates for kids and seniors, too. Call 800-387-6200 or 906-635-5241.

And you must visit the Museum Ship Valley Camp, a massive 1917 steam-powered freighter whose cargo hold and other decks boast the "largest Great Lakes maritime museum." You get to walk the decks and peek into cabins of the captain, mates, and sailors off this vessel, as well as the mess hall, galley, and pilothouse, which offers panoramic views of the lake.

But perhaps the most popular exhibit is harbored in one cavernous space in the cargo hold: a lifeboat from the *Edmund Fitzgerald*. It is eerie to see this fragile vessel, agonizingly torn and crumpled by the ferocity of the storm that sunk the legendary ship. And as you read the accounts or view a video that reviews the final hours of this tragic shipwreck, the display becomes even more terribly sad. Call 906-632-3658.

Look Around the Clock

26

Lighthouse Legacy

When people think "Midwest," they often imagine flat fields filled with neat rows of corn, soybeans, and other breadbasket crops. While this perception might be on the mark for some states, it's all wrong for Michigan.

Just a glance at any map reveals that Michigan is at the heart of the Great Lakes, among the world's largest inland lakes. Four out of the five Great Lakes surround the state's two peninsulas with about 3,200 miles of shoreline. That's more than the entire East Coast. And when you're traveling in the Wolverine State, you're never more than 85 miles from one of Michigan's Great Lakes.

Since Michigan served as the heart of Great Lakes navigation since the 1600s and the hub of its shipping industry since the mid-1700s, it's not surprising that scores of lighthouses sprouted like wildflowers along its long blue shorelines. On the Great Lakes, where jagged shoals, narrow inlets, and dangerous shorelines can snag ships for deep-sea graveyards, lighthouses have always been a signal of safe passage.

Of the state's 116 remaining lighthouses and navigational lights, fewer than 30 remain open as historic museums or accessible to the public. So if you want to visit Michigan's lighthouse legacy, here are some of the best choices.

Upper Peninsula

More than 40 lighthouses line the shores of the Upper Peninsula on Lakes Superior and Michigan. Whitefish Point, north of Paradise, has boasted a light since 1849 to lead ships past its rock-infested shores (nicknamed "graveyard of the Great Lakes"). Since the early 19th century, more than 300 shipwrecks have occurred in an 80-mile stretch of open water from Whitefish Point to Pictured Rocks. Despite improvements in navigation lights, ships continue to founder here.

Consider the legendary *Edmund Fitzgerald*, an iron-ore freighter that disappeared in Lake Superior in 1975; Canadian folk singer Gordon Lightfoot eulogized the tragedy with a tune that still brings tears to the eyes of sailors everywhere. You can learn more about that shipwreck, and other legend and lore of the Great Lakes, by visiting the Great Lakes Shipwreck Museum in Sault Ste. Marie.

The museum is located under a light tower that dates to 1861, when it replaced the original beacon. It's an eerie memorial to the brave men and women who worked the Great Lakes near these treacherous waters. Models of boats now sitting at the bottom of Davy Jones's locker are displayed along with artifacts collected from those wrecks, including a ship's bell from the 1897 schooner *Niagara*. A quarter-hour movie on Great Lakes shipwrecks adds to the atmosphere. Of particular interest is a huge light-beacon lens, with an explanation of how light is reflected by its 344 crystal prisms, and the bell from the famous *Edmund Fitzgerald*. For more information, contact Whitefish Point–Great Lakes Shipwreck Museum, 111 Ashmun, Sault Ste. Marie, MI 49783, 906-635-1742.

While roaming these parts, head to the nearby Museum Ship Valley Camp (see Chapter 25) for a

Summer

glimpse of one of the few artifacts ever recovered from the *Edmund Fitzgerald*: a lifeboat apparently shredded by the furious waters that claimed the freighter.

The brick tower of the Point Iroquois Lighthouse and Maritime Museum, owned by the U.S. Forest Service and located near Sault Ste. Marie, dates to 1870. Visitors can climb 65 feet to the top and tour the lightkeeper's residence. Contact Point Iroquois Lighthouse & Maritime Museum, Bay Mills Township, Hiawatha National Forest, Sault Ste. Marie Ranger Office, 400 I-75 Business Spur, Sault Ste. Marie, MI 48783, 906-635-5311 or 906-437-5272.

Why just visit a lighthouse when you can overnight in one? The Big Bay Point Lighthouse, built in 1896 to guide ships plying Lake Superior on their way to the Keweenaw, is one of only two lighthouses in the United States that act as bed-and-breakfasts. Owners John Gale and Linda and Jeff Gamble offer seven rooms (five with private bath) to travelers who'd like to experience the thrill and tranquility of keeping a navigation light on land's end. Climb the light tower to get panoramic views of Lake Superior and the Huron Mountains. Or, from the inn's back door, follow three-mile-long hiking and cross-country ski trails into pristine wilderness.

The working lighthouse, open year-round to overnight guests, gained notoriety more than 30 years ago when it was selected for a "principal role" in Otto Preminger's renowned film *Anatomy of a Murder*, based on a crime committed near here.

Adding to the mysterious surroundings is the lighthouse's ghost, said to be that of the first lightkeeper, who was found hung from a nearby tree. Guests have heard the sounds of jangling chains and seen curious, unexplained shadows in the middle of the night. (There may be no better "spooky quotient" in the Midwest.) Big Bay is located about 30 miles north of Marquette. Contact Big Bay Point Lighthouse, Box 3, Big Bay, MI 49808, 906-345-9957.

Lighthouse Legacy

Lower Peninsula

Port Huron claims Michigan's oldest surviving lighthouse—the Fort Gratiot Light, an 86-foot-tall tower that has been flashing warnings to ships since the middle of the 19th century. Perched on the shoreline of Lake Huron, the lighthouse park includes an 1874 lightkeeper's red-brick house and a turn-of-the-century Coast Guard station. There are also great views of passing freighters navigating the swift current of this narrow inlet. Contact Fort Gratiot Lighthouse, Garfield Street at Omar Street, Port Huron, MI 48060, 313-984-2424 or 313-982-3691.

Also in Port Huron, in Pine Grove Park, is the Lightship Huron Museum. The curious 97-foot-long boat is one of several now retired lighthouse ships that anchored off the shoreline and provided "automated" beams of safety for pilots of passing ships. The *Huron*'s light is said to have been detectable from more than 14 miles away. Contact Lightship Huron Museum, Pine Grove Park at the St. Clair River, Port Huron, MI 48060, 313-982-0891. For lighthouse information, call the Port Huron Area Chamber of Commerce, 810-985-7101.

Whitehall claims one of the quaintest settings for a lighthouse. Its historic White River Light Station, built in 1875, offers fabulous views of Lake Michigan's sand dunes along the coastline. The lighthouse museum is filled with ships' relics and artifacts, including sextants, charts, foghorns, models, and photographs. But its most prized possession may be a life ring from the *Edmund Fitzgerald*. Contact White River Light Station Museum, 6199 Murray Road, Whitehall, MI 49461, 616-894-8265.

Summer

27

Living-History Ramble

MACKINAW CITY

MANY WEEKENDERS ARE IN SUCH A HURRY TO HOP A FERRY that'll carry them over to the historic sites on Mackinac Island that they overlook two fabulous living-history museums on the shorelines of Lakes Michigan and Huron.

But listen closely as your museum guide begins the story of the region.

"Fort palisades, shoreline campsites, forest trails, and pioneer homesteads echo voices from the past, voices speaking Chippewa and Ottawa, French and English. They reverberate with exciting tales of long ago: the Native Americans who revered the land as it nurtured them, French paddlers who were the first European explorers, an international fur trade that thrived for more than a century, the British challenge to the territory and trade, the struggle and triumph of the American Revolution to gain control of these strategic crossroads."

The days of long ago come alive at Colonial Michilimackinac and Mill Creek, living-history museums that transport visitors back into North American history.

Any weekend during the season is a good one to visit Colonial Michilimackinac, an 18th-century French fur-trading village and military outpost located in Mackinaw City. But if you come over the Memorial Day weekend during the annual Fort Michilimackinac Pageant, you'll see a vivid and moving snapshot of history right before your eyes. Here's what I saw:

British Redcoats are in a panic behind the walls of the fort, which guards the Straits of Mackinac at the crossroads of the Great Lakes. Chief Pontiac's attacking braves are lofting arrows at their enemy. Cannon and muzzle-loading rifles thunder as soldiers try to beat back the Indians. Finally, Pontiac enters the fort and captures the hated English commander. The chief considers his attack a fitting retribution for mistreatment under the British.

The action continues during the festival, one of the oldest historical pageants in the country. It features more than 500 actors outfitted in authentic 18th-century costumes and uniforms as they reenact the 1763 battle on the very spot it took place.

But even on nonpageant days, Colonial Michilimackinac uses costumed interpreters, live demonstrations, restorations, reconstructions, and continuing archaeological excavations to depict 18th-century life on this erstwhile fur-trading post built in 1715 by the French, but later occupied by the British.

On guided walking tours, you might meet the likes of Ezekiel Solomon, Michigan's first Jewish settler; trader Henry Bostwick; and Ojibwa chiefs Minevana and Matchekewis. Redcoats fire muskets, fur traders tally pelts, women stir supper pots, and voyageurs swap stories of their rollicking river adventures.

Especially interesting are cannon firings on the lakeshore, musket firings and drills, blacksmithing and woodworking demonstrations, and the boisterous arrival of fur traders, who enter the fort's gates carrying their cache of hard-earned pelts. You can even attend a traditional French wedding in the fort chapel.

Special children's programs include visits with a British soldier, missionary priest, and village homemaker. Kids will learn French songs, learn about colonial wildlife, and see how the nature of everyday chores has changed over the years.

You also can glimpse inside an 18th-century Native American encampment along the shores of Lake Michigan, where interpreters in traditional dress share native lore of the fur trade era.

Two additional attractions shouldn't be missed: walk through an archaeological tunnel to view original artifacts in layers of earth, just as they came to rest hundreds of years ago, and watch ongoing archaeological digs for more of the hidden treasures that provide the historical foundation for the village's continuing reconstruction.

Then head to Mill Creek State Historic Park, near the shores of Lake Huron about three miles southeast of Mackinaw City. The reconstructed 18th-century water-powered sawmill, nestled in a 625-acre nature park, offers visitors a chance to see early American resourcefulness in action.

Most exciting is the sawmill demonstration, when the whir of the saw biting into fresh logs replicates the work once done by settlers who provided Mackinac Island with finished lumber. My daughter Kate still remembers when she was chosen to help another "settler" by grasping the handle of a long saw and grinding through a huge log. "This is hard work, Papa," she said after a few minutes on the job.

Later we hiked over some of the three miles of forest trails, through a demonstration tree farm of hardwood and aspen, past a large beaver pond, and to scenic overlooks. We also saw a reconstructed sugar shack. On guided treks, the park's naturalist identifies plants and points out the habitats of forest creatures.

Throughout the year, these historic parks, along with Fort Mackinac on Mackinac Island and Mackinac Island State Park, provide a quartet of thrills for visitors wishing to rediscover northern Michigan's colonial roots. Special events are also part of the fun. Besides the Memorial Day pageant at Colonial Michilimackinac, schedule your visit to enjoy these major festivals: Mackinac Island's Lilac Festival in early June; Fourth of July at Fort Mackinac; and the French Colonial Feast and Twilight Tour at Colonial Michilimackinac in late July.

FOR MORE INFORMATION

Admission is charged at individual state historic parks; a money-saving combination ticket is also available. The season lasts from mid-May to mid-October. Contact Mackinac State Historic Parks, Box 370, Mackinac Island, MI 49757, 906-847-3328; before May 15, call 616-436-5563.

Summer

28

Freedom Festival

DETROIT AND WINDSOR

DETROIT IS ONE OF THE FEW U.S. CITIES THAT LOOK SOUTH into Canada. Park-filled Windsor, Ontario, just across the Detroit River, can be reached by a short drive over Ambassador Bridge or through the Detroit-Windsor tunnel.

For three decades, these international neighbors have jointly celebrated their countries' independence days—Canada's Dominion Day on July 1 and our Fourth of July—during a massive two-city, two-week-long bash. Called the International Freedom Festival, it's the largest international summer festival in North America. More than 100 mostly free events take place on both sides of the Detroit River, underscoring the peace and friendship existing along the world's longest unguarded border. In fact, nearly three million people stream to the fest each year.

If there's one Freedom Festival event you shouldn't miss, it's the free fireworks extravaganza. This spectacular show alone draws more than 750,000 people annually who'll watch eight tons of fireworks shot from two barges anchored in the Detroit River, midway between Detroit and Windsor. Riverside gazing sites go quickly, but you can gather at either Hart Plaza in Detroit or Windsor's Dieppe Park for a good view of the fireworks and other entertainment throughout the evening. Rain dates are always slated.

Another hightlight is "A Fort Night" at Historic Fort Wayne, one of the best-preserved Civil War forts in the Midwest. Located about three miles from downtown Detroit, the history-packed show features music from the U.S. Army Volunteers and Windsor's Scarlet Brigade bands. You'll also be treated to the Pennsylvania Rifle Regiment, a fife and drum corps dressed in colorful hunting-frock uniforms, the Windsor Police Pipe Band, and an explosive cannon salute at the evening's end.

The Canadian Armed Forces' "Snowbirds" or other precision-flying wizards often jet through some amazing aerobatics during airshows (usually held on July 4) at Windsor Airport. The daredevil pilots synchronize their airborne tricks while traveling hundreds of miles per hour. Sometimes the shows conclude with a bonus: a fabulous flyover by menacing World War II "war birds" and bomber planes. You'll get a chance to see the planes close up—and even sit in some of the cockpits—at a ground display preceding each show. Admission is charged.

On July 1, Windsor's Canada Day parade stretches along Ouellette Avenue beginning at midmorning. It claims to be the largest parade of its kind in North America, with floats from both Ontario and Michigan, scores of marching bands, streetside entertainment, and more.

Cover your ears from the roar of hydroplanes skimming over the water of the Detroit River at speeds surpassing 180 MPH during the Spirit of Detroit's Trophy Races. More than 500,000 people cram the shoreline to watch these speed monsters race over the two-mile course. General admission tickets and special seating boxes (which include food and snacks) are available.

Other Freedom Festival events might include the Canadian Film Festival; Monte Carlo Casino at Windsor's Cleary Auditorium, featuring blackjack, wheels, Nevada tickets, and other games of chance; a grand carnival, with rides, carny foods, and midway; Arts-Alive entertainment in Windsor, often featuring the likes of Toronto's Second City National Touring Company, opera, classical and choral music, drum corps competitions, street dances, new citizens' swearing-in ceremonies in both Detroit and Windsor; and much more.

FOR MORE INFORMATION

Many area motels offer "Firecracker Specials," with lodging package rates. Contact the Metropolitan Detroit Convention and Visitors Bureau, 100 Renaissance Center, Suite 1950, Detroit, MI 48243, 313-259-4333 or 800-338-7648.

Freedom Festival

Fall

29

Campus Crawl

ANN ARBOR

How would you like to see what New England looked like almost 10 million years ago—crammed with camels, rhinos, elephants, and rats the size of wolverines?

Or marvel at masterpieces by the likes of Rembrandt, Cézanne, Monet, and Miró?

Personally, I get the biggest bang out of touring one of the country's first nuclear reactors built in the post-war period.

But whatever your preferences, you'll probably find something to enjoy during a campus ramble around the University of Michigan in Ann Arbor, which offers all of the above and more.

This beautiful campus is almost a self-contained city, crammed with museums, art galleries, great record and book stores, cafés, restaurants—even one of only eight presidential libraries in the country (Gerald Ford's). Its colorful student body makes for interesting people-watching. And if you visit during football season, you can step inside America's largest college sports stadium (capacity 101,000 people) to watch the Michigan Wolverines challenge other Big Ten schools on the gridiron. That is, if you can get your hands on some tickets, which are sometimes harder to find than a snowball in Hawaii.

You've got lots of room to roam. There's the main campus, newer North Campus, and all kinds of geographic nooks and crannies crammed with interesting shops and curios. Serious exploring is up to you.

For a *China Syndrome* kind of thrill, don't miss tours at the Phoenix Memorial Laboratory on Bonisteel Boulevard. This two-megawatt nuclear reactor, built in 1957, was only the second reactor constructed after World War II. It is devoted to peaceful uses of nuclear energy; these include teaching, product testing, medical research, and experimentation. Authorities claim that no classified government work is done here.

The reactor runs on a fixed cycle of 10 days at full power followed by four days of shutdown and maintenance, so be sure to call ahead for tour schedules.

Fall

While on tour, you'll see all kinds of strange-looking instruments, rods, and contraptions contained in reinforced concrete rooms that look more like bunkers. Especially mesmerizing is a blue glow from demineralized water in the center of the reactor. But not to worry—it's said you could drink the water out of there . . . though I've never seen any volunteers. You'll see the control room through a thick panel of glass; technicians monitor the reactor operation with a control board crowded with buttons and dials. Another thrill is the "hot caves," small rooms encased in three-foot-thick protective glass and lead-shielded doors, used to handle radioactive material. Call 734-764-6220.

The University of Michigan Exhibit Museum, on Geddes Avenue, is one of the kids' favorite spots—although my younger daughter, Dayne, cringes when we walk through seven dioramas that depict prehistoric insects the size of Buicks. Imagine a dragonfly with a 30-inch wingspan; giant roaches (think Florida); and a Los Angeles area filled with sabertoothed tigers. (Today, of course, L.A. offers another flourishing species—the Hollywood shark.)

Kate, my older daughter, can never get enough of the dinosaur exhibit, with massive skeletons depicting "monsters" that roamed from Montana to Utah more than 150 million years ago. Especially loathsome (and "really neat," says Kate) are the bones of the allosaurus, a cannibalistic creature with sharp claws and long, sharp teeth. Call 734-764-0478.

My wife, Debbie, always heads to the University of Michigan Museum of Art on South State. There she finds masterpieces by some of the world's most celebrated artists including Cézanne, Rembrandt, Whistler, and others. Another of her favorite stops is its gift shop, which offers an especially handsome collection of folk art and handmade jewelry. Call 734-747-2067.

Lunchtime can only mean one thing—Zingerman's Delicatessen at Detroit and Kingsley. Noodle kugel, homemade coleslaw, corned beef Reuben, New York cheesecake. Call 734-663-3354.

Not far from the deli is Kerrytown, its restored 19th-century buildings filled with more than 30 shops and a farmers' market. Browse, work off your lunch, maybe buy yourself some fine wine for a later celebration.

Also nearby is Domino's Farms, headquarters to Domino Pizza founder Tom Monaghan. It includes a classic car museum, Frank Lloyd Wright museum, Eskimo artifacts, and a petting farm for kids.

If you're an artsy kind of person, visit during mid-July for a special treat: the annual Ann Arbor Art Fair, which draws more than 400,000 people to the booth-filled "Diag," the greenbelt cutting through the UM campus. You'll browse among the handiwork of all kinds of craftspeople, among them painters, woodworkers, and sculptors. In fact, count on about

1,000 exhibitors at one of the largest street fairs in the country.

Treasures carry all kinds of price tags. My last time here, I saw handmade pottery mugs for as little as $5 each; then again, some of the finer art, including intricate sculptures, sold for thousands of dollars.

For More Information

Contact Ann Arbor CVB, 120 West Huron, Ann Arbor, MI 48104, 734-995-7281 or 800-888-9487.

Fall

30

Apple-Picking Paradise

EAU CLAIRE

HERB TEICHMAN IS AN APPLE MAN TO THE CORE.

His 600-acre family farm, Tree-Mendus Fruit, grows more than 200 apple varieties. That includes a "Museum Collection" orchard of varieties, grown from seed, that represent the same kinds of apples that were favorites of people like Benjamin Franklin.

And he can spin tales about the apple kingdom for hours at a time. Wanna talk Japanese apples? How about Limbertwig? Maybe you're curious about the origins of apple names?

"You know how the Red Delicious apple got its name?" Teichman told our "Fruit Safari" wagon tour as it rolled through the orchard during harvest time. "In the mid-1800s, an Iowa farmer named Jesse Hyatt used to throw apple peelings to his chickens, peelings that he got from wild apple trees. Apparently, seeds in the peel sprouted a tree in his chicken yard. He thought these new apples looked a little strange. Not rounded like most, but with five bumps on the bottom. But they were the best apples he'd ever tasted.

"The farmer decided to enter his apples, which he called Hawkeye, in a fruit show down in Missouri. When the judge took a bite of the apple, he said, 'That is delicious.' And the name just stuck."

Teichman laments that today's bigger, redder, earlier-ripening Red Delicious apples have lost some of the explosively sweet taste of Hyatt's early Hawkeye. However, thanks to Tree-Mendus's museum orchard, you can sample that same Hawkeye and judge for yourself.

"It's not a pretty-looking apple," Teichman says. "And it's got a strange pumpkin color that we're not used to. But it's sweeter than any other Delicious apple you'll ever taste."

You can purchase apples from the orchard's market store, where Teichman often greets visitors and offers samples of apples and other fruits grown at Tree-Mendus. But most opt for a U-pick adventure out among the rows of apple trees.

Apple varieties range from the traditional (Jonathan, McIntosh, and Delicious) to the exotic (the Wolf River apple weighs in at more than a pound). But most crops boast good color, size, and lots of flavor, thanks to Teichman's tender loving care. U-pick prices include half-bushel and whole bushel bags, provided by the orchard. Buy more than two bags, and you get the rest for half price. You can even "rent" your own tree during the growing season and harvest all its bounty for your family. Ask Herb for details.

Apple harvest activities include "Fruit Safari" guided tours through the orchard on wagons pulled by Percheron horses or tractors. Also available are a large family picnic area, a chapel in the woods, and swings for the kids. The market store offers picked fruit and apple cider. And an annual Columbus Day special can't be beat: a whole bushel of apples and a pumpkin for just $14.92.

There's lots more fun: You can escape from muggy city nights to the cool clear air of twilight during the farm's Harvest Moonlight Hayrides; sunset hayrides are also on the schedule. Tree-Mendus can even arrange a cookout to complete your day or evening at the farm; its picnic area includes tables and a shelter in a private area of the orchard. Both families and small groups can rent the space, but it's in great demand, so make sure you call ahead for reservations.

Besides apple harvests, note that Tree-Mendus also grows a variety of other delicious fruits (cherries, peaches, nectarines, plums, apricots, and pears) with harvest times ranging from early July through October.

And if you'd like to help the orchard celebrate more than 20 years of "spit-tacular fun," visit during its International Cherry Pit Spitting Competitions, usually held over the Fourth of July weekend. Each year, finalists in this lip-strong sport hope to spit their way to glory and even earn a spot in the *Guinness Book of World Records*, which recognizes these competitors' splashy accomplishments.

In fact, the North American pit-spitting record is 72 feet, 7½ inches, set by Rick "Pellet Gun" Krause of Sanders, Arizona, in 1988. Compete yourself or just watch the legendary pucker styles of past contests, which include the "Damascus Shotgun Tongue Curl," the "Indiana Rifle Purse," and Krause's own "Perilous Pellet Gun Powershot."

For More Information

Contact Tree-Mendus Fruit, 9351 East Eureka Road, Eau Claire, MI 49111, or call its Ripe 'N Ready hot line, 616-782-7101.

Apple-Picking Paradise

31

Walking with Hemingway

PETOSKEY

"As soon as it was safe for the boy to travel, they bore him away to the northern woods," says the first sentence of Carlos Baker's biography *Ernest Hemingway: A Life Story*.

In fact, Hemingway spent a lot of time "Up in Michigan," fishing "The Big Two-Hearted River," visiting an "Indian Camp," and hunkering down during a storm he called "The Three-Day Blow." Every one of his first 17 summers, beginning in 1900 at one year old, was passed at his family's cottage on Lake Walloon in the Little Traverse Bay region. Hunting and fishing with his father, cutting down trees and working farm fields with friends, and wandering the empty places of Michigan's turn-of-the-century wilderness fueled his imagination and became the raw material that fed his early writing.

Now Hemingway fans have an opportunity to follow "Papa" Hemingway's footsteps during the annual Hemingway Walk weekend, held the third week of October and headquartered at the Perry Hotel in Petoskey.

The weekend starts Friday night with a "readers theater" where selections are read from three Hemingway stories. Selections have included "The Killers," "Soldier's Home," and "Cat in the Rain." A member of the Michigan Hemingway

Society discusses the works, putting them into a historical context of Papa's Michigan days.

Saturday features a narrated boat cruise on Lake Charlevoix, past Hemingway Point to Horton Bay, a village often mentioned in his "Nick Adams stories."

That afternoon, the "Hemingway Walk" includes guided tours of places Hemingway frequented during the summers of his youth. These include the boarding house where he once rented a room (now a private home); Little Traverse Historical Museum, which has an extensive Hemingway collection; and the Perry Hotel, built the year Hemingway was born (1899) and noted in his diaries as an overnight stop during a 1916 trout fishing trip. "Records show that he paid seventy-five cents for a room," noted a spokesperson for the hotel.

On Saturday night, another Hemingway expert comes to the hotel to discuss Papa's works. A few years ago it was Lorian Hemingway, author of *Walking into the River* and granddaughter of the Nobel Prize–winning author; she read from her own book and discussed how the Hemingway legacy has affected her life and work.

Finally, Sunday's activities might include a discussion of "The Big Two-Hearted River," one of Hemingway's most-read stories, and a seminar on fishing offering insights about why it is such an important symbol in the author's work.

If you have some extra time of your own, there's lots of additional Hemingway territory to cover in these parts.

Hemingway described Horton Bay, located about 40 minutes southwest of Petoskey, as "only five houses on the main road between Boyne City and Charlevoix. There was also a white building with a general store and post office, with maybe a wagon hitched out front."

There's no hitching post anymore, but the 117-year-old Horton Bay General Store remains the town's major Hemingway landmark. It's still a fishhooks-and-hardware kind of place, where regulars keep coffee mugs hung on the back wall. It's also one of the surprisingly few places around here that sell Hemingway memorabilia—T-shirts, sweatshirts, and postcards bearing his likeness.

Although Hemingway met his first wife, Hadley Richardson of St. Louis, in Petoskey, they were married at Horton Bay's little Methodist church in 1920.

You also can go down to the edge of the bay, just off the main road, to gaze at the spot where Nick Adams fished and camped in the story "The End of Something."

Driving back out of town past Horton Creek, you can see some cottages along the road that were the setting for "The Three-Day Blow" and "Summer People."

It's also interesting to note that although Hemingway spent much time here, he misspelled the town's name in his published works, calling it "Horton's Bay."

Windemere, the original family cottage built at the turn of the century for $400, still stands on the shores of Walloon Lake. Though designated a National Historic Landmark, the modest summer home is owned by Hemingway relatives and not open to the public. Yet a steady stream of gawkers still come to take a peek at another of Papa's landmarks.

You can fish the lake as Hemingway did, as long as you have a Michigan fishing license. It's still a good fishing hole, according to local anglers.

While there might be a wild river or two around here where you can catch trout with your bare hands, the Big Two-Hearted River isn't one of them. But it's still a good place to canoe. It's located near Seney on Michigan's Upper Peninsula. Many Hemingway scholars say he actually fished the closer-by Fox River, but used the other's name in his stories because it's more colorful.

Walking with Hemingway

During 1919, Hemingway took a room in a boarding house at 602 State Street (now a private residence) in Petoskey, where he no doubt gathered material for "The Torrents of Spring," written in Paris. In this story, characters wander Petoskey streets pondering suicide and chasing a "squaw" clad only in moccasins.

You can eat at one of Hemingway's Petoskey haunts. At Jesperson's, 312 East Howard Street, Papa ate pie and shot the bull. Also stop in at the nearby Park Garden Cafe, where he played billiards.

After Hemingway left the Little Traverse Bay region for Paris in 1921, he returned only once, in the late 1940s. When asked why he hadn't come back sooner, he replied, "I've always been disappointed in places where I've returned. I have such loving memories of northern Michigan that I didn't want them interrupted."

For More Information

Perry Hotel Hemingway Walk weekend packages include two nights' lodging, breakfast Saturday and Sunday, Saturday dinner, all programs, and the boat tour/luncheon. Reservations are recommended; contact the Perry Hotel, corner of Bay and Lewis Streets, Petoskey, MI 49770, 616-374-4000 or 800-456-1917.

32

Curious Kids' Museum

ST. JOSEPH

A FEW YEARS AGO, KATE, MY OLDER DAUGHTER, SAT IN THE anchorperson's chair behind the desk of WKID News. As the camera closed in, her image suddenly flashed on the television screen.

With raven hair and dark eyes, she looked like a sophisticated television personality. (OK, maybe fathers exaggerate a little.) Kate's "newscast" featured the latest on world politics and her commentary on how she hoped the Chicago Blackhawks would start playing winning hockey again so that "my papa won't complain so much after the games."

During the weather segment, Dayne, my younger daughter, stood in front of a U.S. map pointing to Florida and telling anyone who would listen that she's counting on another trip to Disney World this summer.

These were funny, precious moments for us all, and our family still talks and laughs about them. But the TV studio is only a small part of the fun in store for visitors to the Curious Kids' Museum, a hands-on children's wonderland in downtown St. Joseph.

The museum, housed in a vintage building across the street from bluffs overlooking Lake Michigan, opened in 1989. Though not nearly as spacious as similar museums in Chicago or Indianapolis, Curious Kids offers two stories of displays that encourage children to poke, sniff, squint, giggle, listen, pluck, blow, climb, dawdle, or otherwise explore things like dinosaurs, a kid-size ship that "sails" the lake, and most everything else imaginable.

Kate and Dayne were immediately dazzled by a life-size picture of Michael Jordan, still their favorite basketball player, which was tucked just inside the front door. "Wow, he's even taller than you are, Papa," Dayne said. Kate went looking for a similar cutout of Sammy Sosa, her most recent Chicago Cubs heartthrob. "No luck," she reported back.

The first major display is the "Global Child" room. Kids can walk into kitchens from all over the world and play with hands-on exhibits that teach them about the richness of world culture and cuisine.

Nearby, Kate also enjoyed a "build-a-fish" computer that encourages children to use their imaginations in creating new fish with weird shapes and other strange characteristics.

In "Kidspace," the girls joined other tots in face painting. Dayne put on a puppet show that attracted an audience of at least a dozen other children. And almost everyone climbed onto a fancy carousel horse.

"Kids Port" is a good place for children to expel some of their manic energy and excitement. The tall-ship mock-up allows plenty of climbing and sliding, and there are seamen's rubber boots and hats to wear so kids can feel like real sailors as they hoist sails, fly flags, and "cook" meals in the ship's galley.

I had never seen an albino frog, but that's what was resting in an aquarium tank in the "Discovery Room." There are also plenty of Lake Michigan fish swimming around, as well as geology displays, environmental videos, microscopes, and more.

Upstairs, the girls dashed to the bubble machine, which enveloped them in a long bubble from head to toe. Then they played at a contraption that uses strobe lights to "freeze" shadows to walls, where they end up looking like early caveman paintings.

Another highlight is the giant mirrored kaleidoscope chamber. After Dayne crawled inside the box, she yelled, "Hey Mama, I see a million Daynes."

Not a big hit with our kids was "Body Works," a display filled with X-rays, medical-school-type plastic body parts that can be taken apart to discover internal organs, and Mr. Bones, a huge skeleton whose hands and legs move. Dayne summed up her feelings best: "Yuck!"

Other display areas include "Soundworks," where you can play pipes and tap toes on a floor piano like the one featured in the Tom Hanks movie *Big*, and a machine exhibit that boasts everything from pendulums, whirling gears, reaction-time devices, and washing machines to cranes and flushing toilets.

Maybe the most meaningful exhibit on the second floor is devoted to a greater understanding of people with handicaps. Kate struggled in a wheelchair over bumps, door sashes, and metal grates. "I thought riding in a wheelchair would be really fun," Kate said. "But this is hard work. How do little kids do it?"

Meanwhile, Dayne tried crutches on for size. "Papa, remember when you had these after your broke your foot playing hockey?" I said I remembered. "Well, don't do it again, okay?" she added.

All other fun notwithstanding, I still believe the television studio is the most exciting attraction for kids. I even dare moms and dads to resist seeing how they look on

Curious Kids' Museum

the tube. (And take solace in the fact that TV adds about 10 pounds to your normally svelte frame.)

The museum also offers science enrichment workshops for kids of all ages. But whether you come for an entire afternoon of fun, for special classes, or just as a respite on a long drive home from western Michigan, you and your kids will have a blast.

FOR MORE INFORMATION

The museum charges adult and children's admission fees; there's free parking in the museum lot. It's open year-round, Wednesday through Sunday. Contact Curious Kids' Museum, 415 Lake Boulevard, St. Joseph, MI 49085, 616-983-2543.

Fall

33

Spaced Out in Jackson

AN 85-FOOT MERCURY REDSTONE ROCKET READIED IN FLIGHT position stands in front of a massive gold geodesic dome. Inside are some of the nation's most significant NASA artifacts from our outer space explorations, including one of only 20 existing rocks brought back from the surface of the moon.

This isn't Florida's Cape Canaveral or Houston's Mission Control Center. It's the Michigan Space Center in Jackson, only an hour's drive from Detroit.

What is a space museum doing in the middle of Michigan? Jackson is the hometown of four astronauts, more than any other city in the country. The list includes Jim McDevitt, commander of the Apollo 9 mission and Gemini programs; Jack Lousma, Skylab's commander in the early 1970s; Allen Bean, fourth man to walk on the moon; and Al Worden, who flew to the moon as part of the Apollo 15 mission. All have donated personal effects from their outer space travels, which along with NASA's contributions—space capsules, lunar rovers, Saturn 5 rocket engines, satellites, space food, stereo photographs, and more—render the center's appeal literally "out of this world."

The Space Center houses $35 million in space artifacts, including the Apollo 9 Command Module, Mercury and

Gemini spacecraft, space suits and helmets, photos of the moon taken by Neil Armstrong, and the grid floor of Skylab. There's even an exhibit that explains something I've always wondered about—how astronauts go to the bathroom. You'll discover that John Glenn (the first astronaut in space) wore diapers—diaper rash was a real problem. Don't worry. Things are a lot more sophisticated today.

Visitors can trace the history of spaceflight from the early rocket theories of physicist Robert Goddard, to the rockets developed for Nazi Germany during World War II by Werner von Braun, to plans for space settlements. Also on view are space suits worn by the Mercury, Gemini, and Apollo astronauts (it took two hours to dress with full equipment), and you can try on actual astronaut helmets and cooling garments (made with hoses designed for cold running water). Or you can see yourself in a simulated lunar landscape, or even sample some space food. The Space Center has sold more than 6,000 packages of freeze-dried Neapolitan ice cream, though some say it "tastes really chalky."

Other exhibits explain black holes (collapsed stars) and changes in gravity, and offer an up-close look at the Gemini simulator used to train astronauts on that mission. There's also John Glenn's computer control console, a NASA moon rover mock-up, and a tribute to the space shuttle era, including a *Challenger* memorial.

Displays on space technology spin-offs are especially interesting. There are 3,000 products used daily that are direct spin-offs from NASA. "People critical of our space effort often don't realize the breakthroughs NASA has made to get to outer space," a museum official said.

Some of the innovations include heart pacemakers; orthopedic surgical drills that evolved directly from Black and Decker battery-powered drills used to gather lunar core samples; advancements in soles and cushions in athletic shoes,

Fall

from moon boots; digital technology, including watches; Teflon; computer games; and much more.

NASA predictions should interest space buffs—future missions could see increased medical research. (Medical breakthroughs in outer space owe much to zero gravity, as proven by experiments on Skylab flights.) The new medical technology will be used first to operate a manned space station, then maybe to colonize the moon (by 2005?), and to populate Mars 10 years later.

Yep, those are big plans. Requiring big budgets.

NASA also plans to call for manufacturing plants to be established on the moon, for processing asteroids mined from other planets. The new materials would be shipped back to earth.

We'll see.

Of special interest to this writer are plans to develop the X-31, a cross between a conventional jetliner and the space shuttle, by the beginning of the 21st century. The aircraft will travel at 17,000 MPH, enabling me to circle the entire planet in one hour. Now that's a weekend ramble I can't wait to write about.

FOR MORE INFORMATION

The Michigan Space Center is located at Jackson Community College, 2111 Emmons Road, Jackson, MI 49201. Admission is charged; there also is a family admission charge. Open summer, Tuesday through Sunday; winter, Wednesday through Sunday. Call 517-787-4425.

Spaced Out in Jackson

34

Goose Gawking

FENNVILLE

THEY ARRIVE EVERY AUTUMN IN SPECTACULAR FASHION. LONG
V-shaped wedges of honking Canada geese, appearing like
straggly black ribbons wafting crazily in the starkly blue
fall sky.

Sometimes so many Canadas fill the air that the birds literally block out the sun, a great black cloud casting a giant
shadow on the farmscape below. Eventually they circle, drop
softly onto harvested croplands and spongy sedge, and begin
to rest from their long journey.

Their stopover is Todd Farm State Game Refuge in Fennville, autumn home to more than 300,000 Canada geese that
rest here on their annual migration from summer nesting
places along the shores of Hudson and James Bays to win-
tering grounds in southern Illinois.

The spectacular autumn show began in the 1930s when
Canada geese began visiting an Allegan County farm owned
by the Todd family. At first, only about 1,000 Canadas
stopped here during spring and fall migrations. But "word"
must have spread about the prime rest-stop conditions of
the farm and its surroundings, graced with plenty of open
water and unharvested grain, and nestled between Lake
Michigan's white-sand beaches and the Allegan State Forest.

Soon thousands of Canadas touched down on the homestead, creating a majestic sight for bird-loving spectators.

In 1949, the Michigan Department of Natural Resources purchased the farm; in subsequent years, federal excise tax dollars on the sale of arms and ammunition, and Michigan hunting license fees, allowed the DNR to purchase additional farms adjoining the Todd spread. Eventually, it established a 4,000-acre waterfowl management area, along with a 1,300-acre wildlife refuge.

While flocks of geese arrive at the refuge annually beginning the second week of September and stay until early February (after they've been sufficiently nourished for the long journey ahead), prime goose-watching season usually falls from the end of October through early November.

Two species of geese dominate at the refuge: the Interior Canada Goose, in flocks that split between those that stay at the farm during mild winters and others that fly on to southern Illinois lakes and marshlands; and the Giant Canada Goose, which nests in Michigan (and other Midwest states) and flies south only during extremely harsh winters.

Goose-watchers should note that the black-necked birds usually stay on the refuge during daylight hours; at night, the geese head out to nearby open waters. So your best chances to see the geese in majestic flight are at dawn, when the birds are returning to the farm, and at sundown, when they're leaving.

Also note that there are several wetlands nearby that attract large segments of the Todd Farm goose population, offering good viewing and observation areas. These include Potowatomie Marsh and Hutchin's Lake to the north of the refuge, Ottawa Marsh to the northeast, Swan Creek Highbanks Refuge Marsh to the east, and Crooked Lake Refuge to the southeast.

The Todd refuge also attracts a variety of other birds. The list of feathered friends includes snow and blue geese, Ross

Fall

geese, white-fronted geese, all kinds of ducks, bald and golden eagles, and peregrine falcons. Other wildlife residents include deer, pheasants, rabbits, and more.

If you'd rather enjoy a boisterous, honking good time at the refuge, come here during Fennville's Goose Festival, held annually the third weekend in October. "Goose days" include goose trophy contests, wild-goose chases, Mother Goose story hours, loose-goose trolley rides, goose parades, goose cooking, goose dances, and goose-calling contests.

While you're in the area, take a detour a few miles west of Fennville on State 89 to Crane Orchards, family owned since the 1870s. Its apple pie made from scratch—"rolled, crimped and vented by hand"—is among the Midwest's tastiest. You can even purchase a fresh-baked or frozen pie for take-home treats. And kids will love the cidersicles— cider with a little honey added, frozen on a stick.

For More Information

Admission to the refuge is free. To receive more goose-watching information and a Goose Festival schedule of events, contact Fennville Area Chamber of Commerce, P.O. Box 28, Fennville, MI 49408, 616-561-5550.

Goose Gawking

35

Sweet Home Chicago

COLDWATER

WHEN I'M TRAVELING THE MIDWEST RESEARCHING MY TRAVEL books or digging up a story for my *Home & Away* magazine column, I'm often lucky enough to have at least one member of my family tag along.

Sometimes it's wife Debbie and the kids, Kate and Dayne. More than occasionally, grandma and grandpa climb into the minivan and join in the fun. And my brother, Mark, is another enthusiastic traveling companion.

But my Pa is probably my most frequent Midwest traveling companion, especially when I'm on assignment midweek during the school year. And I'll never forget one trip we took together, exploring southern Michigan.

That's when Pa, who's in his 70s but still a very handsome and agile man (big and strong as an ox, too), discovered the Chicago Pike Inn. He's never stopped talking about the place.

Located in Coldwater, the Chicago Pike Inn, a luxurious bed-and-breakfast, is a spectacular house built in 1903. Its exterior features four tall white columns in grand Greek Revival style, and a long veranda ("porch" for us homegrown Midwesterners) perfect for sittin' and rockin' away a lazy summer day.

Owned by Jane and Harold Schultz, along with daughters Becky and Jody, the inn has been carefully restored to reflect its early 1900s grandeur. Guests are greeted in a magnificent reception room, itself elegant with a double-manteled cherrywood fireplace adorned by genuine Staffordshire dogs. In the center of the house is a sweeping cherry staircase leading to upstairs guest rooms; I half expected Rhett and Scarlett to glide down the stairs.

Jane greeted us, and after introductions all around, we headed to the library, where an unusual "whitewood" woodwork is very elegant. After Jane filled us in on some inn history, Pa settled into a wingback chair next to a roaring fire and immersed himself in his reading. I continued a house tour with our hostess, complimenting her on a spectacular restoration.

"It's such a grand house," she said. "Restoring it is kind of our legacy to the community."

The rest of the inn reflects Jane's impeccable selection of antiques, fine art, and fabrics. I discovered leaded Bradley and Hubbard lamps, Schumacher and Waverly wall coverings, fluted cherrywood columns, hand-carved antique furniture, stained-glass windows, wood parquet floors—the list of elegant flourishes seemed endless.

Pa had finished his reading, so we headed to our guest rooms. The inn has six, all with private bath. (A television and telephone are available on request.) It was blissfully peaceful, and after a long day on the road, both Pa and I just wanted to revel in the quiet luxury.

And these guest rooms are exquisite. I had the good fortune to draw Ned's Room, with bold red-and-paisley wall coverings, huge brass bed, and green leather wingback chair that give it the feel of an exclusive gentlemen's club. Pa chose Charles's Room, an interesting Victorian retreat that revels in the period's fascination with Chinese stylings; he looked absolutely regal lounging in his huge sleigh bed framed by a wall canopy.

We both slept soundly, waking the next morning to the sounds of chirping birds. Pa called me over to take a look at the Grandchildren's Room, decorated in pink and furnished with twin iron-and-brass beds, lots of white Victorian-era wicker, and at least 11 antique portraits of darling little girls hanging on the walls.

"Boy, Katie and Dayne would love to sleep here," Pa said. "Can you imagine them in those beds? They'd look like little dolls."

Spoken like the proud, dedicated grandfather that he is.

The morning sunlight sent shards of color through the inn's stained-glass windows. We continued our impromptu tour. It led us into Miss Sophia's Suite, a two-room enclave complete with hand-carved oak bed, oak-manteled fireplace, Martha Washington chair, and more.

"Look at this," Pa said. "It's got a private balcony, too."

Soon we walked downstairs into an elegant dining room and sat down at a splendid table adorned with sterling silver flatware, fine china plates, and fabulous gourmet breakfast treats prepared by Becky.

"I hope you're hungry," she said while carrying platters full of fancy waffles, New Orleans–style French toast, and other treats to the table. "This is all for you."

Later that morning, we said our goodbyes, climbed back into the van, and headed toward nearby Allen, one of Michigan's premier antique-hunting towns. As we browsed among Victorian dressers, handwoven Oriental rugs, and brass knickknacks, Pa couldn't help repeating, "That's one of the nicest places I've ever stayed. What a terrific time we had."

You bet, Pa. It was a terrific time. And not just because the Chicago Pike Inn is a fabulous place.

But because you were with me.

Sweet Home Chicago

For More Information

Room rates include a full breakfast. There are two-night minimums on special weekends throughout the year. The inn is open year-round. Golfing, boating, swimming, cross-country ski and hiking trails, and wineries are nearby. Contact Chicago Pike Inn, 215 East Chicago Street, Coldwater, MI 49036, 517-279-8744.

Fall

36

Pictured Rocks

MUNISING

"HEY, PA? WHERE ARE THE PICTURES?" ASKED DAYNE, MY younger daughter.

Well, that's the first thing many visitors notice about Pictured Rocks National Lakeshore: there are none. You've got to use your imagination.

Maybe the name, Pictured Rocks, came from the Native Americans who lived here long before European explorers entered the region. The first time it actually appeared in print was in Longfellow's poem "Hiawatha." Or perhaps it's a version of a name used by French missionaries and adventurers who named some of the 200-foot-tall cliffs and rocks looming above the shoreline.

Regardless of how it got its name, Pictured Rocks may be the most incredible stretch of Michigan shoreline in the entire state. The craggy, tree-topped rock formations carved by frost and wave action extend more than 40 miles from Munising to Grand Marais. They show an amazing array of shore-cliff features: sea arches, thunder caves, stack cliffs, and other promontories with names like Miners Castle, Chapel Rock, and Indian Cave.

Yet it's the shoreline's "painted" sandstone caves that are responsible for the lakeshore's name. Mineral seepage flows down the cliff faces and oxidizes, causing rainbow hues.

Sometimes the colors and resulting "pictures" (you can imagine just about anything you like) change daily. Other times, a hard rain will wash colors away, and the process begins all over again.

Both painted caves and other unusual rock formations can be seen on three-hour narrated scenic cruises over Lake Superior waters; they're conducted by Pictured Rocks Boat Cruises. To make your float most enjoyable, arrive early to claim a seat on the ship's top deck; it fills up quickly, and it's the best on-board spot to view the incredible scenery. Late-day summer cruises are best for spotting colors because sun glare is reduced.

One of the first landmarks the boat tours pass is Grand Island, a 15,000-acre isle open to campers and hikers. And on the island's eastern shore rests the picturesque "Old Lighthouse." Built in 1867, this wooden structure's light last guided a ship through the narrow straits around the turn of the century. (After all, water here is 229 feet deep!) The lighthouse is owned jointly by owners of a few summer homes nearby who keep it looking like an old lighthouse.

Miners Castle has no connection to mining. It simply was named after one of the first men to live in this area. This craggy, double-spired rock outcropping begins a series of sandstone cliffs that have eroded into fantastic, otherworldly shapes. It's also the only point along the Pictured Rocks lakeshore that is accessible by car, with an observation platform perched 90 feet above the water. Legend says that Father Marquette "preached to the Indians from this point as they gathered in their canoes below."

Caves of the Bloody Chiefs are shallow sea caves where native legend says war-party leaders placed their prisoners so the sea would batter them against the stone walls, killing them.

Rainbow Cave actually drips moisture throughout the year, occasionally forming rainbows. And its rock mineral content is so high, rainbow colors form on icicles during the winter.

Explorers in the 1800s discovered huge amphitheater-like rooms in the caves of Grand Portal. Today, because of the furious storms that come to Lake Superior beginning each fall, they're only a remnant of their former selves. But still mighty impressive.

The 175-foot-tall escarpments called Battleship Row (because their sharp, pointy features resemble the stern of those ships) receive the most furious pounding from Lake Superior's angry waters. In fact, that stupendous wave action is what carved out these remarkable formations.

All of Pictured Rocks' colorful rock formations, estimated to be 500 to 600 million years old, so impressed geologists and other earth scientists that they became the nation's first designated (and protected) National Lakeshore in 1966. They should be part of any Upper Peninsula sight-seeing.

FOR MORE INFORMATION

Admission is charged. Boat cruises run from June through mid-October. Contact Pictured Rocks Boat Cruises, Box 355, Munising, MI 49862, 906-387-2379.

Pictured Rocks

37

Fall Color Caravan

As soon as the hillsides shimmer with the fiery blaze of autumn hues that mantle the broad shoulders of Michigan's maple, oak, and sumac forests, legions of leaf peepers seek out rustic roads, rugged bluffs, and tree-studded shorelines in pursuit of color-drenched foliage.

You can climb aboard this color caravan in several ways. Autumn expeditions by land, water, or air offer chances to gaze at colorful foliage in pristine surroundings. And if you're willing to branch out from your traditional color haunts, I'll go out on a limb and make a few suggestions.

First let's get to the root of the matter. Michigan's traditional peak-color season is mid-September to late October, with colors usually appearing earliest in the Upper Peninsula and latest in the Lower Peninsula's southernmost region. Fall colors depend on chilly temperatures (short days, cool nights), sunshine, and average amounts of moisture to produce peak hues. Lots of rain, freezing temps, or killing frosts can short-circuit Mother Nature's color timetable.

Since weather is so unpredictable, I urge leaf-lovers to call Michigan's fall-color hot line, 800-543-2937, for the latest color reports.

Now that you know when to go, here are the highlights of the hows and wheres:

By Land

Some say the Upper Peninsula's 10 million acres of wilderness are "where autumn comes each year to recharge its colors." Arguably, the Midwest's best autumn hues can be found on the Keweenaw Peninsula in the western U.P.

The 12-mile-long Brockway Mountain Drive, highest point of land between the Rockies and the Appalachians, may be the most renowned fall-color drive this side of Vermont. At the roadway's overlook, you'll view an unbroken bed of autumn shades in the sprawling wilderness of Porcupine Mountains State Park, along with several tree-surrounded inland lakes and streams. Another BMD escarpment overlooks the Lake of the Clouds, sitting 500 feet *below* your vantage point. And views of Lake Superior's dark blue waters, crashing with autumn whitecaps, clash with rainbow hues of primitive pine-green forests that appear on every horizon.

More U.P. color-tour favorites include forested drives on County 513 (north of Bessemer), which heads north of Lake Superior passing seven waterfalls, Big Powderhorn Ski Area, and Copper Peak Ski-Flying Hill—where you can hop aboard an elevator for a hilltop vista of three states, Lake Superior, and Canada.

In the eastern U.P. near Newberry, head to a view made famous in Longfellow's "Hiawatha"—Upper Tahquamenon Falls State Park. Hearty visitors can scale 100 steps to a platform at the brink of the 48-foot-tall falls for more spectacular views.

A color hot spot in the Lower Peninsula is the Lake Michigan shoreline in the northwest portion of the state. Following the coastline from Holland to Harbor Springs, mixtures of hardwood and evergreen forests stand in stark contrast to the backdrop of Lake Michigan's emerald waters. Especially noteworthy is U.S. 131 to Petoskey, which offers tall hills and sweeping views of Bay View and Little Traverse Bay;

Fall

Charlevoix, with several shoreline parks perfect for color gazing and Petosky-stone beachcombing; and the Glen Haven area, with stunning views from 150-foot sand dunes at Sleeping Bear Dunes National Lakeshore.

The 100 miles of Lake Huron shoreline (Bay City to St. Clair) along Michigan's "Thumb" (the east-central portion of the state) offer more color surprises, including tall tree-topped bluffs, historic lighthouses, and wind-whipped sand dunes.

Or head to Michigan's Fruit Belt (see Chapter 9) in the southwest of the state, which snuggles up close to Lake Michigan. U-pick fruit farms (the finest is Tree-Mendus Fruit in Eau Claire; see Chapter 30), the wineries of Paw Paw/Kalamazoo, and lakeside resort towns such as New Buffalo, Union Pier, South Haven, and Saugatuck offer lots of activities surrounded by autumn color.

Especially enjoyable in these parts is the forest drive along State 63, which follows Lake Michigan northeast from Benton Harbor to Blue Star Memorial Highway, and continues north.

By Water

One of the best ways to see color-coated shorelines is by booking passage on the tall ship *Malabar*, a 105-foot, two-masted, gaff-rigged topsail schooner sailing out of Traverse City. Its majestic rigging is guaranteed to remind you of sleek Great Lakes shipping schooners that once roamed these waters by the hundreds. And its 22-foot beam and 100 tons ensure a comfortable motion on the high seas for old salts and landlubbers alike.

The *Malabar* sails from late May to early October, offering everything from high-noon floats to sunset sails. If you'd like a complete sailing experience, reserve a room on the ship, which also serves as a floating bed-and-breakfast. It has accommodations for 21 people in eight private staterooms furnished in mid-1800s windjammer style. Each offers wooden bunks, electric lighting, and a wash basin. Moored about 800 feet offshore, you can either sleep the night away in your room or grab a deck pad and dream under a canopy of stars. Contact Traverse Tall Ship Co., 13390 West Bay Shore Drive, Traverse City, MI 49684, 616-941-2000.

By Air

Many pilots will tell you that the fall color season is probably their favorite time of the year for skyjinks. You'll agree after gliding about 2,000 feet off the ground and taking in all the splashy hues, as well as seeing deer and other wildlife wandering in and out of the forests and woods below.

For altitude without motion, try riding in a hot-air balloon. Passengers in the balloon's gondola don't perceive motion as they glide with the wind over color-tinged forests. Remember that departures depend on weather, and the fall flying season can be shortened by early rainfall. For a list of Michigan balloon pilots and more fall-color information, contact Michigan Travel Bureau, P.O. Box 3393, Livonia, MI 48151, 800-543-2937.

38

Turkeyville USA

MARSHALL

THOUGH THE ROAD SIGN READS "TURKEYVILLE USA," you won't find this town on any Michigan map. But keep checking. Wayne Cornwell has gobbled up legal papers and giblets of information, vowing to convince local politicians that his slice of Americana is worthy of official recognition by Rand McNally and other mapmakers.

In the meantime, let's talk turkey. Specifically, a Cornwell turkey, produced on the historic 150-year-old Marshall farm of Wayne and Marjorie Cornwell, whose special feeding formula yields a succulent tom perfect for holiday dinner tables.

"Grandpa's secret formula is a special milk-grain feed that makes the birds juicier and very tasty," said Patti Cornwell, one of eight family members who run Cornwell's Turkey House, a renowned southwestern Michigan farm and restaurant. "Once you've had a Cornwell turkey, you'll keep coming back for more."

That must be true, since Cornwell's sells more than 15,000 fresh turkeys for the holidays, offering them about one week before Thanksgiving and Christmas.

"More than you'd pay at your local supermarket," Patti conceded. "But there's no comparison in taste." Many Midwest familes have transformed the trip to Cornwell's for Thanksgiving turkeys into a regular holiday tradition.

And even though Cornwell's turkeys are now raised at a farm in Middleville, the family ensures that strict stock and feeding guidelines are followed to preserve the unique taste of their birds.

Sample some turkey yourself at Cornwell's farm restaurant, offering a complete Thanksgiving dinner anytime of the year. That restaurant business started long ago when Wayne and Marjorie sold turkey sandwiches at a 4-H booth during the local county fair. After scores of people expressed disappointment that they could buy the scrumptious sandwiches only during fair week, the Cornwells opened a restaurant behind their farmhouse in 1968. It consisted of two tables and three milk stools. They made $26 the first day.

Today the restaurant menu, which boasts homemade recipes from Grandma Marjorie's kitchen, includes turkey soup, sloppy toms, biscuits and turkey, turkey pasta salad, turkey and noodles, and a char-grilled turkey dinner. Bestseller remains the self-proclaimed "World's Best Turkey Sandwich": buttered turkey topped with mayonnaise on a homemade bun. Or savor a complete turkey dinner, including homemade stuffing, mashed potatoes, gravy, cranberries, coleslaw, and roll.

Cornwell's also produces its own year-round dinner theater, including the popular "Home for the Holiday" musical revue running to just before Christmas. Filled with old-fashioned Christmas songs and traditions, the family-oriented show is offered 12 times weekly, Tuesday through Saturday.

You can just see the show, or opt for a dinner-show package that includes an all-you-can-eat buffet featuring carved roast turkey, dressing, potatoes, veggies, cranberries, rolls, beverage, and a slice of homemade pie. Since the Christmas show sells out quickly, be sure to call well ahead for reservations.

Turkey-lovers who journey to Cornwell's also can browse through "The Country Junction," a concourse of gift boutiques offering collectibles, homemade ice cream, baked goodies, and turkey products; the Christmas Shoppe, filled with holiday finery; and an Antique Barn.

And kids love the petting farm. Even when the farm is pared down for winter, children can still lay their hands on goats, a donkey, and Bart, a grand champion turkey with multiple victories at the annual county fair. Bart is one of 11 pet turkeys on the farm. "We're quite proud that they've been highly trained to gobble on command," Patti said.

For More Information

To get your holiday bird, order by telephone, specifying bird size; it'll be waiting when you arrive at Cornwell's. Or purchase fresh turkeys during your farm visit; however, not all bird sizes may be available. Overnight shipping is also available, but fairly expensive. Open daily. Contact Cornwell's Turkey House, 18395 15½-Mile Road, Marshall, MI 49068, 616-781-4293.

Turkeyville USA

39

The Auto Barons

GROSSE POINTE SHORES, ROCHESTER, DEARBORN, DETROIT

As Detroit transformed itself into the "Motor Capital of the World" and the automobile industry exploded onto the city scene, great fortunes were made by a handful of auto barons.

The "automotive royalty" that emerged from America's demand for cars celebrated their newfound wealth and soon flaunted it, taking on a lifestyle befitting their elevated status. This included huge estates graced by elegant mansions filled with priceless art collections, intricate Old World workmanship, and ornate furnishings.

Beautiful fountains dotted the landscaped grounds of these estates, which included private ponds, lakes, and secluded harbors. Parties were legend, as auto barons invited society's notables to their homes' elaborate ballrooms, then hosted them overnight in one of the maybe 100 rooms in the estate house.

This world of privilege bespoke an elegance that few have ever witnessed, in an age that will never be repeated. But you can relive this "Gatsby" era by touring four of the majestic homes of the auto barons—and see firsthand how they lived their portion of the American dream.

Lawrence Fisher Mansion

The most startling and fantastic house in all of Detroit belonged to Lawrence Fisher, founder of the Fisher Body Company and playboy of the city's 1920s auto barons.

It has been called "glitz bordering on the garish." No wonder. Inspired by the strange, rambling California "castle" of friend William Randolph Hearst, Fisher's 1927 Detroit riverfront estate is a 50-room mansion featuring ornate stone and marble work, doors and arches carved from woods imported from India and Africa, and rare black-walnut and rosewood parquet floors.

More than 200 ounces of pure gold and silver leaf highlight decorative ceilings and moldings. Priceless European handcrafted stained-glass windows throw colored shards of light on interiors. Black majolica tiles with gold insets can be seen in other parts of the house, along with Corinthian marble columns, Roman tiles, and exquisite chandeliers.

Also note the ballroom, decorated to resemble a Spanish courtyard, complete with a cloud-filled "sky" and stars once projected by a light machine.

Fisher is reputed to have had a few bizarre habits, including eating with his dogs (they ate from solid silver bowls) at the dinner table. So it's interesting to note that this mansion continues its off-center history: it's now owned by the Hare Krishnas, who've pretty much maintained its architectural integrity—except for the life-size statue of their late guru sitting in an upstairs room.

Edsel Ford House

The Edsel, named after Henry Ford's only son, may have bombed as a car. But Edsel Ford grew up to become a shrewd automaker like his father; in fact, Edsel became president of Ford Motor Company, taking over when he was only 25 years old.

He built this example of elegance and graciousness on 87 acres overlooking Lake St. Clair. The main house, built in 1929, is designed in English Cotswold style, a large rambling mansion cut from English stone, with limestone hallways and classic designs that resemble European manor homes of the 18th century.

Inside the mansion, note fine examples of 16th-, 17th- and 18th-century English paneling. Original art includes masterpieces by the likes of Cézanne, Matisse, and Van Gogh. There's even a casual Art Deco–style "Modern Room" tucked in among the formal quarters; it was a favorite gathering place of Edsel, wife Eleanor, and their four children.

But the manor house is only part of the estate's astounding beauty. Its lakeside setting is magnificent, as is the landscape design by famed architect Jens Jensen. Also note the "playhouse," another Cotswold cottage, built to a child's scale for daughter Josephine. It's still probably worth more than most of our real homes.

Henry Ford Estate

Fair Lane, Henry Ford's Dearborn estate, entertained some of the most famous names of the era: Charles Lindbergh, the Duke of Windsor, President Herbert Hoover.

Ford convinced friend Thomas Edison to create a six-level power plant that generated enough electricity to make the estate self-sufficient in power, heat, light—even ice-making.

The house itself, built in 1914, is a combination of Frank Lloyd Wright's "prairie style" architecture and European baronial designs—strange until tour guides tell you that Ford switched architects in the middle of construction.

The house is a mixture of formal rooms, handsome hand-carved woodwork, and stately grandeur. Most of the original furnishings have been sold by Ford heirs, and part of the mansion holds offices of the University of Michigan at Dearborn. But you'll still get a peek at some of the mansion's elegant legacies, such as the exquisite woodcarving, and eight different fireplaces with Ford's personal philosophies, like "Chop your own wood and it will warm you twice!" carved into some of the stone edifices.

To get a better idea of the grandeur in which the Fords lived, walk the terrace paths along the Rouge River, where Ford and wife Clara walked listening to the whitewater cascade the automaker built into the stream; imagine Ford and close friend Harvey Firestone stopping to chat by the water. Or follow Ford's favorite walk down Jensen's meadow to a hidden pond surrounded by a peaceful forest.

Also extravagant were Clara's gardens, grottos, and tea-houses, through which she led hundreds of the country's garden clubs. Especially noteworthy are the remains of her formal Rose Garden, once considered among the most beautiful in the world. In Clara's time, more than 10,000 rose plants were tended by over 20 full-time gardeners. Today, similar garden maintainence would cost almost $500,000 annually.

Matilda Dodge Wilson Estate

In 1907, John Dodge married Matilda Rausch, a young Canadian farm girl who had moved to Detroit. And when Dodge died suddenly at age 55, he left a fortune to his wife and family, which she transformed into Meadow Brook Hall in suburban Rochester.

Completed in 1929 at a then-fantastic cost of more than $4 million, this 100-room Tudor mansion remains one of the finest examples of residential architecture anywhere in the world. The home shows all the trappings of wealthy auto-baron stylings (priceless art, ornate woodcarvings, elegant furnishings) without overstating. Matilda donated the estate to Oakland University, and it is now part of the campus.

FOR MORE INFORMATION

Contact Fisher Mansion, 383 Lenox, Detroit, MI 48125, 313-331-6740; Fair Lane, Henry Ford Estate, 4901 Evergreen, Dearborn, MI 48128, 313-593-5590; Edsel Ford House, 1100 Lake Shore Road, Grosse Pointe Shores, MI 48236, 313-884-3400 or 313-884-4222; Meadow Brook Hall, Matilda Dodge Wilson Estate, Oakland University, Rochester, MI 48063, 313-370-3140.

The Auto Barons

40

Wine Country

PAW PAW AND KALAMAZOO

WINE IS A BEVERAGE THAT CONJURES UP MANY VISIONS.

Some recall almost Dionysian pleasures—soft candlelight, good food, Frank Sinatra on the stereo, the sparkling eyes of your special someone.

Another vision is of perfectly cultivated vines arranged in long straight rows, attended to by the gnarled hands of bentbacked peasants working a magnificent centuries-old chateau in French wine country.

Or, just maybe, you think about Kalamazoo.

Okay, so Kalamazoo is not one of America's 100 most romantic cities. Nor does it in any way re-create the Gallic flavors of Provence.

But just as in France, the business of grapes is very important here. Because this is the heart of southwest Michigan's 12,000-acre wine country, and Michigan ranks fourth among the wine-producing states of America. In fact, it has produced scores of award-winning vintages.

One of the best times to visit wine country is during the Kalamazoo/Paw Paw Wine and Harvest Festival held annually in early September. More than 250,000 people come to this "nectar of the gods" celebration to enjoy free vineyard and wine-tasting tours, sample more than 30 Michigan wines, browse through an arts and crafts fair, and watch live entertainment at Kalamazoo's Bronson Park.

Paw Paw, about 15 miles west of Kalamazoo, boasts two of the state's largest vineyards. St. Julian Wine Company, founded in 1921, is the oldest and largest producer of Michigan wines, claiming 36 vintages; call 616-657-5568. Warner Vineyards, started in 1938, has more than 3,000 acres devoted to French hybrid vine cuttings and also claims the Midwest's only champagne cave (fermentation done in the classic French style); call 616-657-3165. Tours of both vineyards explain wine pressing, fermentation, aging, and blending; free wine tasting, too.

At Tabor Hill Winery in Buchanan (about five miles east of Bridgman), you can stroll through rows of trellised vines, some still bearing ripening grapes. Then sample some of its notable Classic Demi-Sec, which has been served to heads of state at official White House functions.

Another way to enjoy wine country is by riding in the leisurely Vineyard Classic Bicycle Tour, which rolls along selected routes through the hilly countryside. (There are both individual and family ride rates.)

But wine tasting is only part of the festival fun. Head to Kalamazoo's Bronson Park for scores of ethnic food booths, art fairs, a country fair, live entertainment, and a grand parade.

If you really want to get into the festival spirit, enter the grape-stomping contest, slated twice during the fest in Paw Paw. There's a nominal entry fee, and prizes go to the winners.

Of course, just about anytime is a good time to visit Michigan's wine country. Here are a few more wineries that you can sample during your ramble through the vineyards:

- **Fenn Valley Vineyards, Fennville** Located about 45 miles northwest of Kalamazoo, this vintner has been a leader in low-alcohol or lite wines, with nine different labels, including a champagne. Self-guided tours of the 230-acre vineyard include a video about the wine-making process. Call 616-561-2396.

- **Lemon Creek Winery, Berrien Springs** They've been growing grapes on this 300-acre spread since the 1850s. Its Chambourcin won a Gold Medal at the 1992 American Wine Society national competitions. And you can even pick your own wine grapes here. Call 616-471-1321.

For More Information

Contact Greater Paw Paw Chamber of Commerce, Box 105, Paw Paw, MI 49079, 616-657-5395; Kalamazoo County Convention and Visitors Bureau, 128 North Kalamazoo Mall, P.O. Box 1169, Kalamazoo, MI 49007, 616-381-4003; West Michigan Tourist Association, 136 East Fulton, Grand Rapids, MI 49503, 616-456-8557.

Wine Country

Winter

41

Loving the Luge

NORTH MUSKEGON

WATCHING TELEVISION COVERAGE OF THE OLYMPIC WINTER Games can put lots of crazy notions inside a person's head. Goofy stuff, like riding the luge.

So here I am, challenging the 600-meter luge run at Muskegon State Park's Winter Sports Center in North Muskegon.

Most people can't even pronounce luge, the French word for sled. Some say lugeing was born in Switzerland, where winter enthusiasts noticed that little sleds used by Swiss mail carriers to negotiate icy mountain roads would make for exciting sport. Soon ice-slicked chutes with hairpin curves and long straightaways rocketed lugers down a long run, or kunstbahn. Today lugers exceed 70 MPH on Norway's 1200-meter Olympic luge run, a refrigerated concrete tube that cost $15 million to build.

One of the reasons American lugers lag far behind perennial powerhouses like Germany is that we have few places to practice. North Muskegon, whose four-year-old luge run was built by volunteers with $300,000 in materials, has one of only four luge runs in the United States (the others are in Lake Placid, New York; Marquette, Michigan; and Fairbanks, Alaska).

My luge instructor, a 15-year-old named Jimmy, has been lugeing since he was 12. While training here (he's hoping to receive advanced instruction at the Olympic luge run in Lake Placid, with an eye toward earning a spot on a future Olympic luge team), he gave me some simple advice as we checked out body mechanics prior to my first run: "Keep your head down, your feet up, and hold on."

Jimmy explained that it usually takes only subtle movements of the legs and shoulders to "drive" or position the sled, which is four feet long, weighs 30 pounds, and holds lugers six inches above the ice. "To go left, move the right leg toward the left while dipping the left shoulder into the sled, and turning your head to the left," he said. "Do just the opposite to turn the other direction." I told him that the instructions sounded like a riddle. "It takes beginners a little while to get the motion down," he added.

I also discovered that professional lugers memorize the course so they won't have to look up for turns and straightaways, which would increase wind resistance. Just a few thousandths of a second can be the difference between finishing first or last in world-class competition. A glance at the results of recent Olympic luge runs shows that just a few tenths of a second separated several sliders.

With proper training, lugeing isn't very dangerous, despite appearances. Everyone from eight-year-old kids to grandmas in their mid-60s have slid down the run without incident. That excellent safety record is due in part to the presence of two coaches on the run at all times, giving instruction, watching form, and offering tips for safety and improvement. The run also maintains four starting gates; how high up the run you start depends on ability level.

I'm told that only a half-dozen people have ever slid from the very top. Those lugers attain speeds of more than 60 MPH. Beginners start just below two vicious curves so they won't tear up "body and wood" as one instructor put it.

Winter

After donning my helmet and positioning myself on the sled, I knew my moment had come. A small crowd had gathered at the starting gate, and I began to feel the adrenaline pumping. I wanted to make a good run. I especially wanted to avoid an embarrassing run.

I grabbed the handles of the gates, rocked back and forth, and propelled forward. I found it relatively easy to guide the sled through the chute, climbing the walls of a few turns only to shoot out into the final straightaway. The sky rushed by overhead and the speed was exhilarating. I never even hit a wall.

It's best not to become either anxious or overconfident on the luge. Else you'll forget the proper mechanics of maneuvering the sled and bash into the wall while executing a turn, just as I did on my next run.

But by afternoon's end, I felt part of an elite group. After all, a recent sports survey revealed that there are only about 250 lugers in the entire country. So bring on Ivan and the Russian horde. Yeah, the Germans, too. I think I'll be ready to take 'em all in the next Olympics.

Well, maybe not.

For More Information

The luge is open to the public on Friday, Saturday, and Sunday, weather permitting, from December through March. A fee is charged for first-timers; that includes about 20 to 25 runs, sled, helmet, insurance, and coaches. A minimal per-day cost is charged thereafter. Contact Muskegon Winter Sports Complex, 616-744-9629.

42

Flailing and Bailing on the Slopes

THOMPSONVILLE

LISTEN UP, SHREDHEADS. IF YOU WANT TO FLAIL AND BAIL, loft a frontside air, make some handplants, or simply shred and destroy, head to Crystal Mountain Resort, located in Thompsonville, between Cadillac and Frankfort in northwest Michigan.

Crystal Mountain boasts an awesome half-pipe that's totally outrageous. Measuring 300 feet long, it drops in deep so you can really rip the pipe and pitch some air. Or if the pipe's not for you, catch some rush rides on the hills, do a total fake mondo, and carve some snow.

Are you pumped, dudes and dudettes?

Or just confused?

OK, I'll translate. I'm talking about snowboarding, one of the country's fastest-growing winter sports and the newest craze to hit Michigan slopes. A cross between skateboarding and surfing, snowboarding requires riders to balance on a 60-inch-long board (which resembles one wide ski with both feet buckled into the contraption), and rip down the ski slopes to "carve some snow" with the board's metal edges.

However, daredevil snowboarders crave more thrills than that. So Crystal Mountain has constructed a 300-foot half-pipe (similar to concrete half-tubes used by skateboarders) out of ice and snow. The half-pipe allows for all kinds of crazed acrobatics, including "pitching some air"—flying through the air Michael Jordan–style for as long as skill and gravity allow.

No wonder snowboarding, a sport born just a little more than a decade ago, is taking off in the heartland.

Snowboarding certainly can add thrills to the region's relatively tame downhill slopes. It's easy to become bored after snowplowing down 400-foot verticals all day long. But strap yourself onto a snowboard and that pimple of a ski hill can take on Rocky Mountain proportions.

The bad news for snowboarding wannabes is that beginners fall down—a lot. And, because your feet are strapped to the board, that means wrists, elbows, knees, and especially your bottom are going to receive plenty of pounding the first day.

But the good news is that snowboarding is not much more difficult to learn than downhill skiing—just a lot different, according to the experts. Heel and toe pressure controls the board. Once you learn to slideslip (or control the edges) and regulate your speed, you can carve some snow on just about any hill.

Many snowboarding instructors insist they can have you standing upright on a board by the end of one lesson, provided you're aggressive and willing to absorb the physical punishment. To cut down on first-day bumps and bruises, wear wrist guards, elbow and knee pads, maybe even a helmet.

As for equipment, all you need is a snowboard (half- and full-day rentals are available at Crystal Mountain) and a good pair of snug-fitting hiking boots or specially designed snowboard boots. The resort also offers group and private lessons, and kids' group lessons.

It's not just teenage skateheads and shredheads that constitute snowboarding's dedicated disciples. As the sport develops, it's beginning to go past that, with more people in their 30s starting to learn. I've also seen several parents and their kids take snowboarding classes together.

But advanced, hardcore snowboarders are usually teens, a fact that can occasionally cause problems with older, more etiquette-minded downhill skiers. But those problems are dwindling all the time, especially as snowboarding broadens its appeal.

If you'd rather watch than flail and bail, Crystal Mountain hosts official Snow Shredders Association half-pipe, slalom, and giant slalom competitions during the winter.

Hang loose, dude.

FOR MORE INFORMATION

If you own a snowboard, a ski lift ticket will get you onto Crystal Mountain's slopes and half-pipe. The resort's ski season usually stretches from mid-December through early April. Contact Crystal Mountain Resort, M115, 12500 Crystal Mountain Drive, Thompsonville, MI 49683, 616-378-2911 or 800-968-7686; the snow-condition hot line is 800-748-0114.

Flailing and Bailing on the Slopes

43

Snowmobiling Snofari

WHITEHALL

LIKE A THUNDERING HERD OF CARIBOU CRASHING THROUGH the pristine wilderness, hundreds of snowmobiles make an annual ramble over backwoods and forest trails during what may be the largest guided trail tour in the Midwest.

It's called the Snofari, and (weather permitting) occurs during the early part of February in Whitehall, about 20 miles north of Muskegon. The winter festival often draws more than 500 machines that roar in a ferocious ribbon through winding woodland trails near the eastern shore of Lake Michigan. The fest snakes through about 90 miles of trails groomed and tracked by the state's Department of Natural Resources. Tours are led by guides who have been using these trails for years.

Snofari is actually a three-day affair that includes a Friday moonlight trail ride, Saturday hot-lunch trail tour, and a Sunday early-bird mystery ride (where guides decide the route and length of the ride).

To join in the snowmobiling fun, you have to bring your own machine or rent one. But the festive weekend includes more than snowmobiling. Count on cold-season activities like sled-dog races, skijoring (skiers pulled by sled dogs), sprint races, and cross-country contests in nearby Montague, as well as horse-drawn sleigh rides, moonlight Nordic skis, family ski tours, ice fishing, and more.

And best of all, Snofari guided snowmobile-trail tour rides are free.

Area motels offer lodging, but this is a popular weekend—make sure you have reservations before heading to Whitehall.

Of course, you don't have to hook up with the Snofari to enjoy Michigan snowmobiling. The state has more than 4,000 miles of groomed trails, with nearly 2,000 miles in the pristine Upper Peninsula.

And if you're wondering how you're going to get across the five-mile-wide Straits of Mackinac that separates the state's lower and upper portions—no problem. For $1, the Mackinac Bridge Authority allows one snowmobiler and one machine to cross from one peninsula to the other.

Also note that while Snofari requires that you have a machine to participate in the fun, Michigan boasts scores of snowmobile outfitters that rent machines, equipment, and trail maps. (You can gets lists of outfitters from local chambers of commerce and free snowmobile trail maps from the Michigan Department of Natural Resources.) For Snofari information, call 616-893-4585.

If you're wondering where some of the state's other snowmobile hot spots are located, read on:

- For snowmobile races in the "wild," head to Cadillac's North American Snowmobile Festival in early February; call 800-225-2537. To see "on-track racing," visit Sault Ste. Marie's February event, the International 500 Snowmobile Classic, which draws nearly 50 souped-up snomos from across the United States and Canada to its iced-over

Indy-style oval track competitions. It has been called the world's largest Enduro race. Call 800-647-2858 or 906-632-3301.

- The resort-filled Traverse City area offers more than 100 miles of well-marked trails, part of a network of paths groomed by the local snowmobile council to a 12-foot width from early December through March. This is prime snomo-weather country, averaging about 150 inches of snow during the cold season. Call the toll-free snow condition hot line, 800-727-5482, for daily reports of snowmobile trail conditions; you'll also receive a free snomo trail map for your efforts. Among the region's finest snomo "roads" are the Boardman Valley Trail, which winds for 81 miles through Grand Traverse County and the magnificent Pere Marquette Forest; the Bear Lake Spur, a 16-mile roar through Betsie River State Forest; and the Blue Bear, a 45-mile trail northeast of Kalkaska. For Traverse City–area lodging and snowmobile rental information, call 800-872-8377.

Snowmobiling Snofari

- Prime Upper Peninsula snowmobile areas include the Paradise, Munising, and Marquette areas. In some U.P. cities, like Copper Harbor and Grand Marais, you're allowed to ride your snowmobiles along designated city streets.

- For dramatic snomo adventures, try crossing frozen Lake Huron between St. Ignace on the U.P. and Mackinac Island; the icebound "road" is marked with discarded Christmas trees—but do not wander off this trail. More trees mark another snowmobile trail, this an international one, across Lake Huron from Michigan's Drummond Island to Canada's St. Joseph Island.

For More Information

Contact Michigan Travel Bureau, P.O. Box 3393, Livonia, MI 48151, 800-543-2937; Upper Peninsula Travel and Recreation Association, 618 Stephenson Avenue, P.O. Box 400, Iron Mountain, MI 49801, 800-562-7134 or 906-774-5480; West Michigan Tourist Association, 136 East Fulton Street, Grand Rapids, MI 49503, 616-456-8557.

Winter

44

Downhill Thrills

WHEN IT COMES TO SKIING IN THE MIDWEST, YOU CAN FIND best bang for your bucks at Michigan ski resorts. In anywhere from a three- to ten-hour drive from my home in Chicago, I can experience downhill thrills for less than half (or a third or fourth) of a Rocky Mountain high. And some of Michigan's North Country ski areas even offer the feel of big-mountain, high-altitude cruising, thanks to the highest hills between the Alleghenies and the Black Hills of South Dakota.

Here's a purely subjective list of Michigan's top six downhill ski resorts. I can't promise you Hollywood stars, but maybe you'll bump into somebody who once met somebody interesting. At least you'll get darn good skiing.

Best Mountains

Searchmont Resort, Sault Ste. Marie, Ontario

If you think the Midwest has no mountains, you've never been to Searchmont. Just a stone's throw over the Michigan border in Ontario, this North Country ski paradise has

700-foot verticals, more than 300 inches of powder annually, rugged beauty, and challenging big-mountain terrain that will especially please serious intermediate and expert skiers.

From the resort's twin-peak mountain summit, you can eyeball the Goulais River Valley, all craggy rimrock, outcroppings, and cliffs that stretch to the horizon; that alone might be better than any Rocky Mountain high.

The slopes might be better, too. West Peak runs have the feel of out-West open-ski touring, perfect for intermediate skiers. East Peak is expert territory with runs that drop straight down the mountain face.

The resort also encourages beginners with its Ski Excel program; first-timers receive a free one-hour clinic with Searchmont pros.

Rental equipment is available, along with daily lift tickets. Ski packages at nearby motels include lodging, lift tickets, and breakfast. And remember that recent Canadian exchange rates are very favorable to the U.S. dollar.

If that's not enough, there's night skiing and a Children's Centre offering a full range of supervised activities, as well as junior ski lessons. Or take the entire family aboard the fabled "Snow Train" that chugs through Great White North wilderness to the winter beauty of Agawa Canyon. Contact Searchmont Resort, P.O. Box 1029, Sault Ste. Marie, Ontario P6A5N5, 800-663-2546 or 705-781-2340.

Most Upscale Atmosphere

The Homestead, Glen Arbor

A secluded preppie paradise, located just above Sleeping Bear Dunes National Lakeshore on Michigan's Leelanau Peninsula, the Homestead revels in its exclusivity.

The resort's beautiful fieldstone entryway leads to the ski area. Its 14 downhill runs are set against the sapphire blue of Lake Michigan. Two of the newer advanced slopes are Stinking Benjamin and Lady Slipper, both presenting a double fall line through the trees. There's also a new giant-slalom course at the top of White Trillium.

There are plenty of clinics for everyone from beginner to expert. First-timers can "learn to ski private" with a one-hour one-on-one session or opt for group "basic training," a two-hour clinic. Then there are classic racing, telemark, rocket racing—the choices seem endless.

A new children's outdoor play area is adjacent to Monkeyshines, the supervised indoor kids' activity center.

Homestead accommodations are among the most luxurious of any ski resort in the Midwest, and it offers door-to-lift shuttle service for guests. Dining includes classical Italian cooking plus cappuccino, espresso, gourmet specialties, and handmade chocolates.

Rental equipment is available, along with all-day lift tickets. Ski packages include "Tip or Tail": two nights' lodging in the Village, two breakfasts for two, a dinner for two, and lift tickets. A new bed-and-breakfast ski package includes two nights' lodging, two breakfasts for two, and lift tickets. Contact The Homestead, Woodridge Road, Glen Arbor, MI 49636, 616-334-5100.

Downhill Thrills

Best Family Resort

Crystal Mountain Resort, Thompsonville

The perfect spot for families that schuss together is located in the heart of Michigan's snowbelt, about 28 miles southwest of Traverse City. It has 23 slopes, 13 lighted for night skiing, and a vertical drop of 375 feet.

Worried about snow? Forget it. Crystal has 35 snowguns capable of pumping out more than 10 tons of snow per minute on 97 percent of its skiable terrain—including, for the first time, two popular beginner trails.

About 60 percent of the guests are families, not surprising since there's something for everyone. There are four kids' programs: Piglet's Place, infants to age three, offers supervised care and activities in a homelike environment; Mountain Midgets, for preschoolers, supplies indoor preski instruction and protected outdoor terrain; Crystal Kids, ages five to ten, includes personalized ski classes, hot-chocolate breaks, and other fun; and Hot Shots, for preteens and teenagers, showcases snowboarding, the hottest new thing on the slopes.

Expert moms and dads might tackle the Gorge, a steep mogul field that offers free-fall glides for the non-faint-at-heart. And the Silver Streak program gives seniors halfprice rates every day on all-day lift tickets.

Later, families can head for the Peak, with its swimming pool, hot tub, and fitness center. Or they can opt for outdoor fun like ice skating, sleigh rides, and more.

Rentals are available, along with daily lift tickets; weekend packages include early-, regular-, and late-season prices. Midweek packages also are available. Contact Crystal Mountain Resort, 12500 Crystal Mountain Drive, Thompsonville, MI 49683, 800-968-7686.

Best Buy

Boyne Mountain, Boyne Falls

You get two mountains of fun when you ski at Boyne. That's because downhill lift tickets are interchangeable between

Boyne Mountain and its sister ski mountain, Boyne Highlands, just a few miles north.

Boyne Mountain offers 17 runs, the longest more than a mile long, and a vertical drop of 500 feet. It also boasts America's only six-person chair lift.

The mountain's steep chutes and mogul fields are a challenge for experts; it's hard to find so many black-diamond (expert) runs anywhere close by. There also are plenty of long, wide, and lazy runs for casual skiers. And you'll never have to worry about snow; it's been rated the country's top snowmaking resort.

Boyne Highlands, near Harbor Springs, offers both bowl-style skiing and trails that resemble Vermont classics. Its vertical drop is 545 feet, but it has 33 runs, a few stretching more than a mile long.

Boyne's best buy is midweek (Sunday through Thursday). Interchangeable two-mountain daily lift tickets are available, as well as two-day lift tickets. Night skiing is offered at both Boyne Mountain and Boyne Highlands, and weekend ski packages are another option. Contact Boyne Highlands, 600 Highlands Drive, Harbor Springs, MI 49740; Boyne Mountain, Boyne Mountain Road, Boyne Falls, MI 49713; or call 800-462-6963.

Best Wilderness Skiing

Porcupine Mountain Wilderness State Park, Ontonagon

Imagine skiing in the middle of a 58,000-acre wilderness tract, surrounded by tall virgin pine trees and views of stacked ice shelves along the Lake Superior shoreline. That's the lure of alpine thrills in the Porkies.

In fact, Porcupine Mountain Wilderness State Park offers primitive ski adventures that'd be hard to beat anywhere else. There's more than 20 feet of snow annually, and daily winter temperatures are on the average 10 to 20 degrees warmer than at inland ski areas. Where else can you climb an observation deck to view spectacular winter landscapes of pristine evergreen forests with Lake Superior as their colorful backdrop?

Oh yes, skiing. The park boasts 11 miles of slopes covering more than 80 acres, with low daily tow rates. Besides seven intermediate trails, there are four black-diamond slopes with vertical drops exceeding 600 feet—among the highest in the Midwest. And one of three beginner trails stretches well beyond a mile.

There's no overnight lodge, but an alpine chalet, located at the foot of the Hiawatha run, offers three fireplaces, food service, ski shop with rentals, and a National Ski Patrol. Contact Porcupine Mountain Wilderness State Park, 599 M107, Ontonagon, MI 49953, 906-885-5275.

Best Local Lore

Indianhead Mountain, Wakefield

If Big Snow Country was good enough for Scarface Al Capone, it should be good enough for you.

I'm not suggesting that the Roaring Twenties kingpin of crime strapped on skis and schussed down hillsides of Michigan's Upper Peninsula, but he and his brother did run a hotel in the area. Nearby Hurley, once a wide-open town and still the Midwest's après-ski mecca, is home to nearly 30 bars, even though its population is only a little more than 2,000.

I doubt if you'll bump into any modern-day thugs at Indianhead, but you will discover a vertical drop of 638 feet, with mile-long runs and intermediate trails galore. They tear through deep pine forests, then play out as wide as a football field, with sweeping turns that direct skiers back to the base lodge.

It also has a ski school, Kinderschule, and Kinderland; lodging includes hotel rooms, trailside condos, and chalets.

Daily lift tickets offer midweek and weekend prices. Midweek lift-and-lodging packages and weekend packages are available. Contact Indianhead Mountain Resort, 500 Indianhead Road, Wakefield, MI 49968, 800-346-3426.

Downhill Thrills

45

Snow Train

SAULT STE. MARIE

IT'S BILLED AS A "JOURNEY THROUGH THE DOMAIN OF THE winter giant"—and that's no exaggeration.

Imagine a world of frozen waterfalls, snow-encrusted mountain cliffs, and ice masses the size of Cleveland. A landscape of snowbound ravines, endless spruce forests, and alpine meadows glistening in winter's mantle like sparkling diamonds.

The adventure starts just across the border from Sault Ste. Marie, Michigan, in its sister town of Sault Ste. Marie, Ontario, and tempts weekend ramblers willing to celebrate the Canadian interior's ruggedly handsome terrain and below-zero temperatures aboard the Algoma Central Railway's annual Snow Train. These winter rail excursions run from early January to mid-March.

You'll be relaxing inside the train's comfortable, heated coach cars, so the only fierce cold you'll experience is when you get out of your auto in the train-station parking lot and walk to the passenger coaches. The rail ramble is also a good deal, money-wise, for Americans, thanks to our favorable exchange rate for Canadian dollars.

Algoma Central officials estimate that more than 10,000 hearty riders hop aboard the Snow Train each year. Leaving its Sault Ste. Marie depot at 8:00 A.M., the train rolls across the Great White North for 114 miles until it reaches Agawa Canyon, a spectacular cold-season reward for nature lovers.

But the trip up to the canyon is just as much fun. Once the "Canadian Soo" and the International Bridge fade from sight, it isn't long before the awe and wonder of a vast wilderness set in. The white of winter is everywhere. Snowdrifts as tall as skyscrapers and pointy icicles the size of Michael Jordan decorate the glacier-scoured terrain.

As the train clickety-clacks along the chilly rails, you'll soon grasp why people said the line's old initials of A.C.H.B. (until 1935, it was known as the Algoma Central and Hudson Bay Railway) stood for "all curves and high bridges."

And you don't have to be an outdoors person to recognize natural landmarks like Searchmont and Bellevue Valleys. Upon boarding, you'll be given a pamphlet that points out scenic highlights that you can spot by finding the corresponding track mile markers.

Easily the most spectacular portion of the ride begins at Mile 102, where the train crosses the frozen Montreal River. It's not just any crossing. This quarter-mile trestle dangles in the crystal air about 130 feet above the river valley.

Once past the river, the train takes a steep descent into the heart of Agawa Canyon, its massive rock walls encrusted in ice. The scenery is otherworldly, and no stops are possible because of heavy snowfall and low temperatures.

On the way back, head to the cozy dining car for a hot lunch or a cold beer. Take your time; the train isn't scheduled to arrive back in Sault Ste. Marie until after 4:00 P.M.

If you can't schedule a special Snow Train tour, hop aboard the Algoma Central's regular rail service any time of the year. It also chugs into Agawa Canyon as part of its normal route; the only difference

Winter

is that you'll have to get off at the canyon to change trains for the return ride home, and there's no food service available.

Hardcore rail fans can travel the entire length of the Algoma Central, a 600-mile round-trip that includes an overnight stay in the French-Canadian town of Hearst. This tour requires at least two days; during cold weather, be sure to bring along your heavy-duty underwear.

For More Information

Admission is charged; there's free parking at the depot. Snow Train reservations are recommended; any remaining seats go on sale at 7:30 A.M. the morning of departure. Call 705-946-7300.

Snow Train

46

Call of the Wild

MARQUETTE

ANY FAN OF JACK LONDON'S *CALL OF THE WILD* CAN CONJURE up visions of hardy sled dogs mushing through the arctic wilderness over immense blankets of snow and ice that cover the Great White North.

But why just imagine dogsledding adventures when you can really do them yourself?

As soon as winter rolls along, just sign up for one of Michigan's dogsledding weekends that can take you through the pristine wilds of the Upper Peninsula. (Contact any one of several adventure outfitters that conduct dog-sledding expeditions to both Upper and Lower Peninsula destinations.)

There is no age limit, and no experience is necessary to participate in these exciting adventures. Using six-dog sleds, guests and gear mush in daylight hours across iced-over lakes and snowy canoe portages. It's easier than it looks, thanks to experienced guides who offer instruction before the expedition gets under way and assist while on the snowy trail.

And here's perhaps the biggest piece of information you will learn out in the wilderness—dogsled drivers never say "Mush."

My wife, Debbie, and I signed up for a dogsledding trip a few years ago. Our guide, Marcel, took us to the nearby kennel where his sled dogs (mostly mid-size malamutes and huskies) yapped and howled while the blustery cold whipped around us.

Marcel explained that sled dogs are trained from an early age. Pups are strapped into harnesses to get them used to the feel, then introduced to the snow. Summer months don't translate into vacations for sled dogs, either. A wooden sled with wheels is used for warm-weather workouts, with increasingly heavy weights piled onto sleds to build up strength.

After choosing the pooches and hooking them up to what looked like a complicated series of harnesses, Marcel positioned us in the sled and off we went along a winding forest trail.

Winter

While the dogs pulled the sled at a surprisingly brisk clip, Marcel explained how to drive the contraption, shifting weight on turns and hills, all the while hollering commands that the dogs immediately obeyed.

Marcel, a ruggedly handsome French Canadian, also seemed to take an avid interest in Debbie. So when it came time for one of us to drive the sled, Marcel suggested that I try first. We exchanged places, and I hopped onto the runners at the back of the sled, gripping the handles and shouting commands to the dogs. Marcel climbed into the sled next to Debbie, pulling the fur blanket over both of them.

I had expert command of the sled while Debbie and Marcel talked incessantly to each other. Marcel barely glanced back toward me. But I didn't mind since this was a *Call of the Wild* adventure come true.

Until we started descending a steep slope. I worked the sled down the incline while we gained speed. Just as I reached a level snowfield (and was about to congratulate myself for a job well done), the sled hit a snow-covered bump and I was thrown off the runners, somersaulting into the air and landing in a heap in a deep drift.

Of course, neither Marcel nor Debbie even noticed that I was no longer piloting the sled. In fact, the contraption continued, driverless, on its merry way until it became but a speck on the horizon.

Then I saw Debbie turn around and point back in my direction, and the sled stopped. Marcel climbed out and returned to his driving duties. When they finally got back to me, Marcel simply said, "I wondered why the sled suddenly felt lighter."

If you'd rather watch these sled dogs in action than pilot a sled yourself, head to one of the biggest doggie trots in the Upper Peninsula: Marquette's U.P. 200 Sled Dog Championship, held in mid-February. The competition draws mushers from all over the northern United States, Canada, and the Scandinavian countries to its 240-mile-long race through snowy forests and across frozen lakes. Another event is the fest's Midnight Run, where dogsledding teams mush 88 miles by moonlight.

FOR MORE INFORMATION

Contact Michigan Travel Bureau, P.O. Box 3393, Livonia, MI 48151, 800-543-2937; or the Upper Peninsula Recreation and Travel Bureau, 800-562-7134.

Call of the Wild

47

Christmas in the Village

DEARBORN

THINK IT'S EASY TO CELEBRATE CHRISTMAS WITH HENRY
Ford, the Wright Brothers, and Thomas Edison? It is, because
they all live on the same street—in Greenfield Village.

The 240-acre outdoor living-history museum in Dearborn, along with the overwhelming displays of historical
artifacts and collections at its sister Henry Ford Museum, is
a monumental testament to American ingenuity, technological innovation, and changing American lifestyles.

It's also a prime showcase for Christmas traditions and
American folklore.

The village includes scores of historically significant buildings collected from all over the country, saved from the
wrecking ball by the foresight and collecting fervor of Henry
Ford. After scouring the nation for pieces of Americana, big
and small, he opened the complex in 1929. Its purpose was
to preserve the country's technological and social heritage.

And a grand opening it was. Notables at the dedication
included Thomas Edison, who reenacted and re-created his
early experiments with incandescent light as part of the
ceremonies.

Ford, who became close friends with the inventor, had
Edison's laboratories moved from New Jersey to this northwest Detroit suburb. Soon the Edison buildings were joined

by many other originals, including the Wright Brothers' 1870 Victorian cottage from Dayton, Ohio, where both lived when they completed their historic flight at Kitty Hawk, North Carolina, in 1903; the Logan County Courthouse, where a young Abe Lincoln practiced law; the elegant 1822 Greek Revival home of Noah Webster; and the Henry Ford birthplace, a modest two-story white clapboard house built by his father in 1860.

During the Christmas season in Greenfield Village, more than two dozen of these historic buildings come alive with the holiday spirit, decorated with yuletide finery while costumed interpreters demonstrate and explain traditional Christmas customs, folklore, cooking, and decorations. Celebrations range from an 18th-century Christmas in the 1748 Connecticut Saltbox House—a frugal celebration because of strictly practiced religious customs—to the elaborate Victorian holiday atmosphere at the Wright Brothers' home.

Other holiday fun includes a hearty Christmas country dinner served in 1880s style at the historic Firestone Farm; displays of antique Christmas cards in the printing office; demonstrations of ladies making winter bonnets in the gaslit millinery shop; a chance to have an old-time portrait taken at the tintype studio; potters and glassblowers demonstrating their crafts; and a tour of the General Store, where kids can play with antique toys.

A special treat is Yuletide Evenings at the Village, an after-hours program that includes candlelight dinners, period musical entertainment, a walking tour or horse-drawn sleigh ride in the village topped off by a welcome mug of hot cider, and more.

Those who wish to stay out of the frosty cold may tour the Henry Ford Museum, itself host to more Christmas activities, including the three-story-high Christmas tree decorated with all the trimmings.

To keep your historical Christmas holiday alive for a little longer, overnight at the nearby Dearborn Inn, a 222-room hotel built by Henry Ford in 1933. Behind "regular" rooms filled with colonial-style furnishings is a village green surrounded by reproductions of five historic American homes in which you can rent guest rooms. The exteriors are of the exact size and materials of homes that belonged to the likes of Patrick Henry, Walt Whitman, and Edgar Allan Poe. The largest is the Henry House, built from the same Virginia brick as the original in Red Hill, Virginia.

For More Information

For dates and schedules of Christmas events at the Henry Ford Museum and Greenfield Village, contact them at P.O. Box 1970, Dearborn, MI 48121, 800-835-5237.

Christmas in the Village

48

Ice Sculpture Spectacular

PLYMOUTH

EVERY JANUARY, CHISELERS FROM AROUND THE WORLD HEAD to this small Michigan town of 12,000 on the western suburban fringes of Detroit.

These chiselers aren't the underworld type, to be sure. But it would be criminal to miss the results of their handiwork—marvelous creations carved from huge blocks of ice.

It's all part of the Plymouth Ice Sculpture Spectacular, a week-long cold-season celebration where scores of winter-ready Michelangelos chip away at more than 400,000 pounds of ice blocks with everything from delicate dental instruments and specialized woodcarving tools to chain saws and sledgehammers. The ice sculptors—some from as far away as Russia, Sweden, Switzerland, France, and Japan—include professional ice carvers, restaurant and student chefs, and amateurs.

Results can include everything from sailing ships 12 feet tall and massive medieval ice castles (one in 1984 measured 30 feet high and 50 feet wide, complete with gargoyles) to towering eagles with wingspans stretching almost 20 feet across. These works of art, and the frozen festival that celebrates them, lure nearly 500,000 visitors to this tiny, quiet town.

Some claim the Ice Sculpture Spectacular is the largest ice-carving competition and display in North America. More than 200 ice statues line the village's main streets; scores more giant ice sculptures sit in Kellogg Park, where most of the festival action takes place. Past displays have included a life-size chess set and a 40-foot-long circus train loaded with elephants, tigers, and giraffes.

During the day, sunlight adds sparkle to the shimmering ice sculptures. In the evening, colored spotlights cast a special glow on the creations.

Individual and team competitions take place over the festival's weekend dates, with carvers vying for awards and prizes. Solo artists work with a single 400-pound block of ice; teams might use as many as 50 ice blocks for their massive displays.

Who knows what these chiselers will come up with next?

FOR MORE INFORMATION

Contact Plymouth Community Chamber of Commerce, 386 South Main, Plymouth, MI 48170, 734-453-1540, or 734-459-6969.

Winter

49

Nordic Pleasures

NOW YOU CAN CROSS-COUNTRY SKI IN YOUR SHORTS, AND you don't have to worry about getting arrested.

That's because a "Revolution" has taken place in Nordic schussing: short skis, only 147 cm long, are replacing the traditional 200 cm–plus skinny boards and injecting new excitement into Nordic touring.

Pioneered by Austrian manufacturer Fischer, micro-ski "shorties" called the "Revolution" were introduced in January 1993. Billed as the "first great learning ski," they've quickly built up a following among cross-country ski instructors and beginner- to intermediate-skill-level Nordic fans.

"The Revolution ski is easier to learn on because it's shorter, easier to turn, and much easier to control on the trail," said Brett Hood, Nordic director at Crystal Mountain Resort in Thompsonville. "Also, the one-size-fits-all Revolution accelerates the learning curve, allowing our instructors to build confidence into first-time skiers faster than ever before."

Even Nordic experts have now given shorties the thumbs-up, noting that they make scaling hills less tiring, are lighter, faster, and "climb and corner like a four-wheel-drive vehicle with a short wheelbase."

Of course, there's nothing wrong with using your old long boards. That's what I hope to do most of this winter while plying Nordic trails at a half-dozen of Michigan's top cross-country ski resorts, listed below.

Short-Ski Paradise

Crystal Mountain Resort in Thompsonville, located in the heart of Michigan's snowbelt about 28 miles southwest of Traverse City, has the distinction of being one of only eight designated Revolution cross-country ski centers in the United States. Here you can rent shorties (Crystal will have 75 pairs on hand) that make it easier to pick up Nordic skills and improve trail speed and stability.

The resort has lengthened and upgraded its trail system, 18 miles of groomed and tracked trails, most winding through forested hills and rolling countryside with terrain for all abilities; it offers more than three and a half miles of lighted trails for nighttime action.

It also has a new beginner's loop, an intermediate trail, and an upgraded "Screaming Eagle" trail, which has earned "extremely difficult" status, with steep downhill plunges, cardiac climbs, and hairpin turns through the trees.

Ski pros at Crystal's Cross-Country Center offer classic diagonal Nordic ski, skating, telemark, and Revolution lessons for beginner to advanced schussers.

There are midweek and weekend/holiday trail-pass prices, as well as family rates; rental equipment is available, with kids 12 and under receiving discounts off trail fees and equipment rates. Nordic packages also are available; children under 17 sleep and ski free midweek when sharing parents' overnight accommodations. Contact Crystal Mountain Resort, 12500 Crystal Mountain Drive, Thompsonville, MI 49683, 800-968-7686.

King of the Canucks

Many schussers agree that cross-country skiing can't get much better than Stokely Creek Ski Touring Center in Goulais River, Ontario. This Nordic paradise, nestled in the shadow of King Mountain (second tallest peak in Ontario) in the pristine Algoma Highlands just north of Sault Ste. Marie, Ontario, offers 72 miles of groomed and tracked trails for classic diagonal cross-country skiing as well as 13-foot-wide skating lanes for more advanced schussers. Many boast mountain, canyon, and lake views.

There are also miles of untracked backcountry trails south of King Mountain for hearty bushwackers.

It's almost always a good season for Stokely. Snow starts early, usually with at least four inches falling in early October. The main lodge continues to be one of the most luxurious in Nordic circles, with its expanded dining room (serving Canadian gourmet meals), fireplaces, saunas, and recreation area. A guest chalet offers four large bedrooms with private baths and a large common room.

Ski packages include a two-day weekend (two nights' lodging and five meals) and a three-day midweek (three nights' lodging, eight meals). Contact Stokely Creek Ski Touring Center, Karalash Corners, Goulais River, Ontario, P0S 1E0, Canada; or P.O. Box 507, Sault Ste. Marie, MI 49783, 705-649-3421.

Nordic Pleasures

Top 10 Haven

Named one of the top 10 cross-country resorts in the Midwest by *Snow Country Magazine*, Shanty Creek–Schuss Mountain Resort in Bellaire offers two separate ski areas about three miles apart, sprawling over 3,400 scenic acres. It has almost 21½ miles of Nordic trails—a few winding between the twin resorts and doubling the fun of cross-country cruising by providing a resting spot at either end of the line.

The full-service resorts, totaling 600 rooms that include slopeside condos, heated outdoor pool, and fully equipped health club, also offer horse-drawn sleigh rides, snowboarding, and downhill thrills in a distinctive Euro-style mix. Daily trail passes, nighttime skiing, rentals, lessons, and weekend packages (two nights' lodging, trail passes, and ski clinic) are available. Contact Shanty Creek–Schuss Mountain Resort, Route 3, P.O. Box 1, Bellaire, MI 49615, 800-678-4111.

Schussing the Dunes

Nordic trails at Sugar Loaf Resort in Cedar wind more than 20 miles through some of northwestern Michigan's most spectacular scenery. But besides the groomed and tracked paths meandering through pristine forests and dipping across hilly terrain, the trails have a big bonus going for them. They access Sleeping Bear Dunes National Lakeshore, a spectacular 40-mile sandswept landscape trail system that presents close-up views of snow-dappled dunes and ice shelves bulging up along the Lake Michigan shoreline.

Sugar Loaf also offers guided cross-country tours, lessons, and rental equipment. Ski packages include a pass good for both Nordic and Alpine schussing. After hitting the trails, come back to the resort for a soothing dip in the indoor pool or whirlpool spa. Or exercise even more in the weight room. Then enjoy a cozy dinner at the resort restaurant, which overlooks the slopes. Contact Sugar Loaf Resort, 4500 Sugar Loaf Mountain Road, Cedar, MI 49621, 800-748-0117.

Family Adventures

At Wilderness Valley X-C Ski Center, near Gaylord, the groomed and tracked trail system sprawls across more than 2,000 acres of wooded hills in the heart of Otsego County's snowbelt, which claims the "best snow in Northern Michigan." Besides state-of-the-art grooming and rental equipment, along with an old-fashioned ski lodge, this Nordic ski haven is especially kid-friendly. Sure, the family can ski together. But if your kids are too young to ski, the center rents "Tur Pulks" (child-pulling sleds) so families can explore more remote portions of the trails together. Chalet overnight lodging is available, with night skiing on weekends. Contact Wilderness Valley X-C Ski Center, 7519 Mancelona Road, Gaylord, MI 49735, 616-585-7141.

Nordic Pleasures

Luxury Schussing

If you want to relax in a world-class resort after challenging some 80 miles of groomed and natural trails, head to Grand Traverse Resort in Acme. The 920-acre award-winning resort features the largest selections of cross-country rental equipment in the North, lessons in classical, freestyle, and racing techniques, a children's ski school, and more. Later, relax in the resort's huge lap pool, whirlpool spa, or weight-training center. Visit the Tower Gallery of Shops, where you can buy everything from fine clothes to Michigan-made souvenirs. And enjoy an elegant gourmet dinner at the Tower restaurant overlooking the snow-covered resort grounds. Contact Grand Traverse Resort, 6300 U.S. 31 North, Acme, MI 49610, 800-748-0303.

50

Ice Fishing Fun

ICE FISHING HAS COME A LONG WAY SINCE THE DAYS WHEN A few hardy anglers huddled and shivered over a hole in the ice on a windswept lake.

Today, you can fish in comfort by renting a portable fishing shanty, having it hauled out over the surface of frozen lakes, and basking inside its cozy warmth. In fact, some of these shanties are downright ritzy—equipped with everything from televisions and stereos to cooking stoves for serving up hot food.

Of course, you still have to auger a hole in the ice and know something about lures such as shiners and fatheads and Pikki jigs. (Unless fishing is just an excuse to hang out with friends.) And a little "fish sense" wouldn't hurt, either. Because anybody can poke a hole in a frozen body of water, but only those "in the know" know about Michigan's real ice-fishing hot spots.

Some of the best include Lake Michigan's Little Bay de Noc, stretching from Escanaba north past Gladstone, which becomes a virtual city on ice, strewn with hundreds of colorfully painted fishing shanties and "ice roads" marked on the water's frozen surface. And along Lake Superior's Munising Bay, which boasts an abundance of coho, Chinook salmon, and trout.

Or maybe you'd rather rub elbows with ice-fishing fans during "Tip-Up-Town USA" in Houghton Lake, an annual mid-January ice angling extravaganza where the sought-after prize is monster northern pike. And during Tawas Bay's annual "Perchville USA," held in early February, when angling for perch (and northern pike) is combined with a hole-in-one ice-golfing tournament and a polar bear swim.

Not only are these places great spots for ice fishing, but they're also the best spots to hear some of the most outrageous fish stories ever told.

You don't have to be a veteran ice angler to enjoy the fun. Weekenders and other newcomers to the sport should contact local bait-and-tackle shops for advice on equipment and shanty rentals. You'll need a fishing license, and some states require an "ice house" license when fishing from shelters. Local chambers of commerce or the state conservation department can give you up-to-date information.

When you do go, make sure you dress in warm layers. A hooded down parka is a must. Long johns are part of the regulation uniform. Warm gloves and insulated, water-resistant boots are essential. And a pair of creepers (spiked shoes) provides a solid foothold on slick ice.

Also keep in mind these ice-fishing safety guidelines:

- Several times a year, ice conditions are dangerous. One is when ice first starts to form and is covered by an insulating blanket of snow; this may result in ice two inches thick in one location, but thick enough to support an automobile just a few feet away. Just before spring breakup, the ice appears "black" when melting snow, rain, and warmer water underneath combine to change its crystalline structure to long needle-like shards that crumble easily.

- Never venture onto frozen big waters without a compass. A sudden blizzard has caused many a confused angler to drive in circles or into open water on a river channel.

- Always cross expansion cracks at a right angle. You'll traverse them faster and much more safely.

- Stick to well-traveled ice roads when using motorpowered vehicles on frozen waters. Don't head off where no one has driven before. Leave that to those who know the lake very well.

That said, all that's left is for you to enjoy your Michigan ice-fishing adventures. And don't say it's hard to find a place for winter angling. With thousands of miles of Great Lakes shoreline, rivers and streams, and 11,000 inland lakes, you have no excuse not to go for it.

231

FOR MORE INFORMATION

Contact Michigan Travel Bureau, P.O. Box 30266, Lansing, MI 48909, 800-543-2937; Michigan Department of Natural Resources, 530 West Allegan Street, Lansing, MI 48933, 517-373-1204; Houghton Lake Chamber of Commerce, 1625 West Houghton Lake Drive, Houghton Lake, MI 48629, 800-248-5253 or 517-366-5644; Tawas Bay Tourist and Convention Bureau, 402 East Lake Street, P.O. Box 10, Tawas City, MI 48764, 800-558-2927 or 517-362-8643; Delta County Area Chamber of Commerce, 230 Ludington Street, Escanaba, MI 49829, 906-786-2192; Munising Visitors Bureau, 422 East Munising Avenue, P.O. Box 405, Munising, MI 49862, 906-387-2138.

Ice Fishing Fun

51

Christmas Holidays

OTTAWA COUNTY

SOME HISTORIANS INSIST THAT FIERCE-FIGHTING HESSIAN soldiers introduced one of the most gentle, enduring Christmas traditions to the fledgling United States of America back in the 1770s.

Besides ruthless battle skills, these German mercenaries (lured here for money proffered by our Founding Fathers to help defeat the British during the Revolutionary War) brought the Christmas tree to America. It was only after they introduced this European custom that festively decorated evergreens became a holiday fixture across America.

That tradition is celebrated annually in Ottawa County (beginning late November and stretching through mid-December), where the nation's Christmas-tree plantation business began in the 1920s. Today, the region still exports more homegrown Christmas trees to the Midwest than any other location in the country.

Communities all across the county get in on the fun with the towns of Grand Haven, Holland, and Zeeland hosting the lion's share of activities.

Grand Haven's "Classic Christmas Celebration" has gaily lighted streets, arts and crafts shows, and a classic-homes guided tour. The downtown Christmas Parade and Tree Lighting, usually held just after Thanksgiving, heralds the official start of the holiday season with the arrival of Santa Claus and his reindeer.

The town's classic-homes tour, usually slated during the fest's second weekend, visits more than a half-dozen dwellings decorated in greenery and holiday finery. Just hop aboard the Harbor Trolley, which provides transportation to all the festive stops. Tickets are required for tour admission.

Also count on a quarter-hour program that tells the story of the first Christmas and showcases a nativity scene with 40-foot-tall figures, scheduled for selected dates at Waterfront Stadium.

Holland, a tidy town settled by immigrants from Holland in the mid-1800s, offers its "Touch of Dutch Christmas," tinged with Old World traditions, ethnic arts and crafts, lively holiday choral programs, and a special Christmas musical pageant. (One of the festival's perennial Christmastime favorites is *Hans Brinker*, or *The Silver Skates*.) It's also fun to go shopping at the town's Dutch import shops, offering unusual holiday gifts ranging from delftware to hand-carved wooden shoes that can even be personalized with your name, a task performed by wood-burning experts.

Another "shouldn't miss" is "Pioneer Christmas" at the DeGraf Nature Center, where you can watch costumed interpreters re-create the holidays of the town's early Dutch settlers. You can help, too, by learning how to dip candles, make corn-husk dolls, and fashion wheat weavings.

Zeeland's main contribution to the festival is "Christmas Card Lane," a street of houses decorated as giant greeting cards heralding the season. But it kicks off its own village celebration in grand style during the festival's first weekend at Main Place Mall; count on caroling, tree lighting, and a parade. (Maps for the "lane" are available from community merchants and the local chamber of commerce.)

Note that Zeeland remains the most Dutch city of the trio; visit here on any day but Sunday, when the strongly religious town literally shuts down. To see some impressive examples of Dutch architecture, take a walk on Church Street (one block south of Main), where there are stately Dutch Reformed churches and solid homes of early-20th-century merchants.

There are also plenty of other holiday shopping areas and special attractions throughout the county, especially in Holland. Manufacturer's Marketplace, just opposite Dutch Village (itself a wonderland of canals, costumes, and wooden-shoed dancers), houses more than 50 factory-outlet stores.

Oh, yes—Christmas trees! Several Ottawa County "U-cut" Christmas tree farms offer a variety of trees, from Scotch pine and blue spruce to white pine and Douglas fir.

235

For More Information

For a listing of hotels, "U-cut" tree farms, and other holiday information, call the Grand Haven CVB, 616-846-8250; Holland Area CVB, 171 Lincoln Avenue, Holland, MI 49423, 616-396-4221, outside Michigan 800-822-2770; Grand Haven–Spring Lake CVB, One South Harbor Drive, Grand Haven, MI 49417, 616-842-4499.

Christmas Holidays

52

Snowshoe Adventures

In the film *Jeremiah Johnson*, greenhorn mountain man Robert Redford can't negotiate the waist-deep snows of the Rocky Mountains. In fact, he's just about stuck; his horse is up to its belly in drifts.

Along comes Will Geer, a veteran mountain man, his grizzly-bear-claw necklace jangling in the wilderness silence as he progresses across the surface of the snow on his snowshoes.

"Looks like you got a problem, pilgrim," Geer says.

Yeah, no snowshoes.

But snowshoes had their own problem, an image problem, until just a few years ago. They were thought of as an exclusive tool of mountaineers, backcountry bushwackers, and North Country adventurers whose extraordinary fitness enabled them to struggle across a blizzard-covered landscape in their unwieldy foot-strapped contraptions.

No more. Mountaineers trudging through the wilderness in search of "grizz" have been replaced by weekend adventurers exploring winter ecology and scenic backcountry vistas on modern snowshoes that are light, easy to use, and require less energy than downhill or cross-country skiing.

In fact, more than 440,000 Americans snowshoed for recreation last winter, thanks to revolutionary technical innovations that have made the sport user-friendly to legions of winter-lovers. Unless you're a purist, forget that old snowshoe of B-movie fame—a huge wooden frame that looks like an oversize tennis racket laced with rawhide in a hexagonal pattern of crisscrosses that straps on your foot but constantly falls off along the trail.

Today's new snowshoes are much different. Most are made of lightweight airplane-quality aluminum, with thick nylon deckboards, secure bindings, and inch-long claws underneath to help grip ice and snow. They also come in a variety of bold neon colors.

Strap on a pair for the first time and you're still likely to feel like an oversize duck with huge webbed feet for a short while. But soon they'll feel completely natural, and you'll be gliding across the snow surface in search of that silent freedom discovered only in hard-to-reach backcountry destinations.

Even if you walk slowly, your snowshoeing adventure will result in a pretty good workout. (It's recommended that beginners be in moderately athletic shape for the best experience.) However, a new sport called "snow running" is emerging, with participants dashing across the snow in specially designed snowshoes that are smaller and lighter (weighing only 40 ounces) than a hiking or backcountry snowshoe. This is an aerobic activity recommended only for those in great shape.

You can buy lightweight hiking or running showshoes at almost any winter outfitter. Of course, you may be one of those people who revel in tradition and want no part of these new aluminum gewgaws. In that case, head to the Iverson Snowshoe Company in Shingleton; this modest Upper Peninsula company is one of only two factories still making wood-frame snowshoes in the United States. Guided tours of the plant reveal how long strips of white ash are steamed and bent to form the frame, dried in a kiln overnight, and handlaced with rawhide or neoprene strips. You can buy yourself a pair of these beauties for around $100.

Now you're all enthused about snowshoeing, but don't know where to go? Any state park, forest, or hiking trail will do. But for guided snowshoe adventures through some of the state's most fabulous wilderness regions, contact Marquette Country Tours, 809 West College Avenue, Marquette, MI 49855, 906-226-6167.

And keep an eye out for those grizz.

For More Information

For information on snowshoe factory tours, contact Iverson Snowshoe Company, P.O. Box 85, Shingleton, MI 49884, 906-452-6370. For more snowshoe opportunities, call the Michigan Travel Bureau, 800-543-2937.

Snowshoe Adventures

Index

243